NOMAD'S HOTEL

TRANSLATED FROM THE DUTCH BY
ANN KELLAND

CEES NOOTEBOOM

NOMAD'S
HOTEL

TRAVELS
IN TIME AND SPACE

A MARINER ORIGINAL
MARINER BOOKS
HOUGHTON MIFFLIN HARCOURT
BOSTON • NEW YORK
2009

First Mariner books edition 2009
Copyright © 2006 by Cees Nooteboom
English translation © 2006 by Ann Kelland

For information about permission to reproduce selections from
this book, write to Houghton Mifflin Harcourt Publishing Company,
6277 Sea Harbor Drive, Orlando, Florida 32887-6777.

www.hmhbooks.com

The English translation of the Rainer Maria Rilke poem
on page 64 is copyright © William Gass
See Publication Acknowledgments on pages 241–242 for a list of
places and dates of first publication of individual selections.

All photographs copyright © Eddy Posthuma de Boer

First published in Great Britain in 2006 by Harvill Secker,
published in Canada in 2007 by Douglas & McIntyre

Library of Congress Cataloging-in-Publication Data
Nooteboom, Cees, date.
[Nootebooms hotel. English]
Nomad's hotel: travels in time and space/Cees Nooteboom;
translated from the Dutch by Anne Kelland.—1st U.S. ed.
p.   cm.
1. Voyages and travels.   I. Title.
PT5881.24.O55N6613   2009
839.31'86408—dc22   2008020813
ISBN 978-0-15-603535-4

Text set in DTL Albertini Custom
Designed by Naomi MacDougall

Printed in the United States of America

DOC 1 2 3 4 5 6 7 8 9

Contents

NOMAD'S HOTEL

Moving Around in One Place: Cees Nooteboom on Travel

Alberto Manguel

"What does that movement signify?"
—Goethe quoted by Schubert quoted by Cees Nooteboom

THE TITLE OF Cees Nooteboom's book of travel writing is all wrong, if it implies that he is in any way a nomad. A nomad is someone who is never in one place. Nooteboom, on the contrary, is in a thousand places. In fact, his defining characteristic seems to be his omnipresence, a quality that, together with an apparent omniscience, he shares with the god of Moses. In that sense, Nooteboom is less a traveling writer than a well-traveled authorial presence.

Robert Louis Stevenson once observed that he did not travel to go anywhere, but to go. "I travel for travel's sake," he said; "the great affair is to move." He had obviously not read *Nomad's Hotel*. Reading through this splendid selection of "travel" pieces (the inaccurate label cannot be avoided), it becomes obvious that movement itself doesn't matter to the author. In fact, it could be said that *Nomad's Hotel* is an empirical demonstration of the truth of Zeno's paradox concerning the impossibility of movement because, as the Greek philosopher famously remarked, to get from A to Z we must first reach the middle point L, and before that the middle point D, and so on and so on. Nooteboom's argument is even less encouraging than

Zeno's: to get from A to B according to his cartography, we must first discover Z, which is seemingly inaccessible, and the pleasures of city C, which remain vague in the memory, and the promises of the town of W, which we may (or may not) one day visit, or miss completely by landing in another, utterly different, place. (This latter event happens to Nooteboom when, instead of visiting the Spanish Sahara, he finds himself in deepest Gambia.) Nooteboom's maps have no roads—only sites in which, by means of his magnifying glass, we can discover a host of tiny buildings, minuscule inhabitants, particular events dazzling in their precision and as revealing as small epiphanies. Nooteboom turns every reader into a vicarious Gulliver in Lilliput.

Out of sheer cussedness, Nooteboom begins his book with a quotation from his great ancestor, Ibn al-Arabi, who, in the twelfth century AD, defined existence precisely as movement. "Immobility can have no part in it," wrote the noble traveler, "for if existence was immobile it would return to its source, which is the Void. That is why the voyaging never stops, in this world or in the hereafter." With a splendid linguistic twist, Ibn al-Arabi confuses our endless movement through time with a pragmatic movement through space. It is true that, even cloistered in one's room for the whole of one's life, one is condemned to travel through the years, hour after hour, as the sundial motto has it, wounding us, until the last hour decrees our death. But movement from one point of this earth to another is merely a succession of moments of being still: our geography exists only in the instant in which we stand upon it, on our own two feet. I insist on applying this Berkleyan view of space to Nooteboom's observations. As Nooteboom himself says in the conclusion of a poem included in his first piece: "A way is away." The corollary is that a place is never away, but here.

It is this constancy of place that lends the tone to Nooteboom's travels. Venice, for instance, the grandest example of a place that is always there, gives the impression to those who reach her for the first time that they already know her and to those who revisit her (as Nooteboom remarks) the keen desire "to approach Venice for the first time again." This, of course, is a literary wish—that of a reader who longs to be once again at the first unopened page of a book he or she loves. Indeed, Nooteboom is a literary traveler par excellence: his baggage consists less of socks and toothpaste than of Dante and Virgil who, like Nooteboom, undertook their journey with a bundle of remembered readings and beloved authors.

Nomad's Hotel is what medievalists would call a "wise book." That said, I suspect the wisdom in Nooteboom's observations is bred less out of seasoned traveling than out of literary experience. To demand "a superlative degree of the plural" for Venice (Paul Morand's "Venices" does not suffice); to know that there are places that "either you leave immediately or you stay for a year. Anything between produces a bad piece of writing"; to wonder whether all the room numbers of all the hotels you've ever stayed in, added up, "contain a coded message" about your destiny and your persona; to call the grass "idiotically green"; to know that not to speak a language turns you "into a very small child, a dog, or a foreign-er—for these three are none of them capable of understanding what you say"; to be strong enough in your aesthetic convictions to leave Mantua in order to turn around and enter the city on foot, merely to see it better—all these are the gestures of a man for whom litera-ture is the true mirror in which the world is reflected. Not so he can escape the world, turn his back on it, but rather to ensure that he is not turned to stone by its power, like Perseus when he faced Medusa. For all true travelers know that the reality of the world distracts from the reality of the world.

As with the best travel books, after finishing *Nomad's Hotel* I was glad that Nooteboom has been to the sort of places that I love discovering but that I feel I'm too old and too keen on creature comforts to visit. Gambia is no doubt on the list of countries in which I'll never set foot, and now, thanks to Nooteboom, I don't have to. In Gambia, pace Nooteboom, I've read Tibullus in the small bed of a rickety hotel, I've rejoiced in "furnace-hot streets" lined with hibiscus and frangipane (I, who hate any temperature above 15°C), I've swum in a tropical ocean (asking myself why Nooteboom didn't fear the possible presence of strange and dangerous fish), I've slept in a ship's cabin on "gray and heavily stained" sheets, I've been woken by the sound of a cockroach "as big as a child's thumb" making crunching sounds "as if someone is chewing on too-long nails," I've waited in dusty bureaucratic corridors in an attempt to interview the Gambian president for no conceivable reason except that of justifying my presence in Gambia. All in all, I've suffered the nightmarish experience of having been hired (as Nooteboom describes it) to act a part in a play "by an African Pinter." And this, without moving from my chair. Movement indeed.

A piece written a few years ago by Nooteboom, on the Aran Islands, ends with a few words that someone says to him and which he carefully copies out: "We ourselves are the only source of meaning, at least on this little beach of the universe. These inscriptions that we insist on finding on every stone, every sand-grain, are in our own hand. . . .We are writing a work so vast, so multi-vocal, so driven asunder by its project of becoming coextensive with reality, that when we come across scattered phrases of it we fail to recognize them as our own." For the reader of *Nomad's Hotel,* many a distant sand-grain, many a stone, now bears a signature in the right-hand corner: *Cees Nooteboom.*

In the Eye of the Storm

"THE ORIGIN OF EXISTENCE is movement. Immobility can have no part in it, for if existence was immobile it would return to its source, which is the Void. That is why the voyaging never stops, in this world or in the hereafter." These words, by the twelfth-century Arabian philosopher Ibn al-Arabi, are from his detailed tract on traveling, the *Kitâb al-isfâr, The Book of Revelations on the Effects of Voyaging,* a mystical and deeply religious piece of writing, in which everything—God, the universe, the soul—is viewed through the prism of movement, and throughout the entire book this movement is invariably referred to as voyaging. I am neither Muslim nor religious, I bought the book in Paris some time ago because it contained the word *voyage* (*safar* in Arabic, plural *asfâr*), because it was a dual-language edition and I love the beauty of Arabic script, and also because, when I flipped through it in that Parisian bookshop, I noticed a couple of things in the introduction that preoccupy all genuine travelers, be they from the twelfth century or the twentieth. The translator and writer of the introduction, Denis Gril, points out that he could have translated the word "effects" with "fruits"—on the one hand to underline the positive outcome of traveling, on the other hand because, due to its origin, the Arabic word for fruit, *natâ'ij*, makes one think of "to give birth," with its evocation of the intellectual, spiritual fruits of traveling. A voyage, says the text, is thus named because it reveals a person's character, or, put more simply, for the benefit of those who travel alone: on a journey you get to know yourself.

Yet another word, *siyâha*, pilgrimage, catches my attention in that introduction, possibly due to my fascination with Santiago de Compostela. Its definition reads: "parcourir la terre pour pratiquer la méditation—i'tibâr—et se rapprocher de Dieu." Traveling around the world, meditating and drawing nearer to God. The latter would be a pretension for me, but substitute the word *God* with *mystery* and I do feel able to subscribe to it. For how do these things come about? One fine day, and I know how romantic and old-fashioned that sounds, but it is what happened in my case, I packed a rucksack, took leave of my mother, and caught the train to Breda. An hour later—you know how small the Netherlands is—I was standing at the side of the road on the Belgian border sticking my thumb in the air, and I have never really stopped since. At that time any meditative thought, any metaphysical pretension was foreign to me, those sorts of things only come later, rather in the way a Tibetan prayer wheel functions in fact, with the movement preceding the thought. To put it in a different way, I never again stopped moving around, and gradually I began to think while doing it, and you could, if you wished, call this thinking meditation.

Two things are significant here: anyone who is constantly traveling is always somewhere else, and therefore always absent. This holds good for oneself, and it holds good for the others, the friends; for although it is true that you are "somewhere else," and that, consequently, there is somewhere you are *not*, there is one place where you *are* constantly, all the time, namely with "yourself." And no matter how simple it sounds, it does take a long time before you become fully aware of this. For there is always the incomprehension of the "others" to contend with. How many times did I have to hear Pascal's dictum, "the root of the world's misfortune lies in the fact that human beings are unable to remain in one room for twenty-four hours," before it began to dawn on me that, on the contrary, I was the one who was always at home, namely with myself. But that traveling self was repeatedly confronted by the stay-at-homes' questions, with one question recurring with monotonous regularity at each interview, so much so that I have lost count of all the fabrications with which I replied. "Why do you travel, why do you travel so much?," followed by (accusingly), "Are you running away from something?," by which they meant and mean, running away from yourself, which for me conjures up visions of a demonic, pathetic, tortured self, forever driving me back into the desert or on to the high seas. The true answer, having to do with learning and contemplation, with curiosity and perplexity, is just not spectacular enough. In 1993 I wrote an introduction to a little book called *De Koning van Suriname* (The King of Surinam). It contains my earliest traveler's tales, written in the 1950s, when I was a seaman, plying the route to Surinam, on the north-east cost of South America. My introduction begins. "Traveling, too, is something . . ."

Traveling, too, is something you have to learn. It is a constant transaction with others in the course of which you are simultaneously alone. And therein lies the paradox: you journey alone in a world that is controlled by others. It is they who own the boarding house where you want a room, they who decide whether there is space for you on the plane that only goes once a week, it is they who are poorer than you and can benefit from you, they who are more powerful because they can refuse a stamp or document. They speak in tongues you cannot comprehend, stand next to you on a ferry or sit next to you on the bus, they sell you food at the market and send you in the right or wrong direction, sometimes they are dangerous, but usually they are not, and all this has to be learned: what you should do, what you should not do, and what you should never do. You have to learn how to deal with their drunkenness and yours; you have to be able to recognise a gesture and a glance, for no matter how solitary a traveler you are you will always be surrounded by others; by their expressions, their overtures, their disdain, their expectations. And every place is different, and nowhere does it resemble what you were accustomed to in the country you come from. That slow process of learning the things I would need later on, in Burma and Mali, Iran and Peru, began then. Not that I was aware of it in those days, I was far too busy keeping myself afloat in a sea of new impressions. I had no time to think about myself, I traveled and wrote like someone who could not yet travel and write. All I could do was observe, and then attempt to circle around what I saw with words. I had no theories about the world with which to test the confusing reality all about me, and everything I could not yet do is manifest in these stories.

Maybe the genuine traveler is always positioned in the eye of the storm. The storm being the world, the eye that with which he views it. Meteorologists tell us that within this eye all is silent, perhaps as silent as a monk's cell. Whoever learns how to see with this eye might also learn how to distinguish between what is real and what is not, if only by observing the ways in which things and people differ, and the ways in which they are the same.

Baudelaire wrote that travelers leave in order to depart, and he also wrote about the spurious notions they take with them, and about the "bitter knowledge" their travels provide them with, about "the petty, monotonous world that allows us to glimpse ourselves, yesterday, today, and tomorrow: an oasis of horror in a desert of tedium." Looked at from this point of view, perhaps it is he who stays at home among the familiar anecdotage of daily life who is running scared, being unable to stomach this bitter knowledge. As far as I am concerned it is not about which of us is the hero here, but about which of us is doing his soul's bidding, at whatever cost.

Once, when I had no way of knowing what I now know, I chose movement, and later on, when I understood more, I realized I would be able, within this movement, to find the silence necessary in order to write; that movement and silence are balanced in a union of opposites. That the world, with all its drama and crazy beauty, its baffling vortex of countries, peoples, and histories is itself a traveler in an endlessly voyaging universe, a traveler on its way to new journeys, or, to put it in the words of Ibn al-Arabi: "As soon as you see a house you say, this is where I want to stay, but scarcely have you arrived before you leave again, in order to be on your way once more." I once wrote a poem about this *way*—the way as destiny, calling, or temptation—that attempts to convey this eternal, cyclical movement. Hence its title.

> "The Way"
>
> I am the way.
>
> Straight as an arrow
> aimed at the distance,
> but in the distance
> I am
> far away.
>
> If you follow me,
> Here, there, everywhere
> You will arrive,
> Anyway.
>
> A way is away.

1996

Forever Venice

PALUDE DEL MONTE, Bacino di Chioggia, Canale di Malamocco, Valle Palezza, how wonderful it would be to approach Venice for the first time again, but this time to steal upon her, rowing toward the labyrinth through that other labyrinth of the marshes, among the marine creatures, in the early-morning mist on a January day like today, with nothing but the calling of birds and the plashing of oars, the brackish water calm and glistening, the vision in the distance still veiled, the city wrapped in her own secrets. Palude della Rosa, Coa della Latte, Canale Carbonera—on the detailed map of the Lagoon the waterways seem to be depicted as waving fronds of weed, as plants with sinuous, shifting tentacles, but they are waterways within the water, ways that you have to know as a fish knows its way, channels within water that becomes land again at ebb, wet land of oozing mud, hunting ground of the spotted redshank, redshank, and sandpiper on their endless quest for worms and tiny shellfish in their abode of water and sand. They were the first inhabitants, and should that city, like a slow-motion *Titanic*, ever sink down into the soggy ground upon which she presently still appears to float, perhaps they will be the last, as if between those two moments the world had dreamed up something that was impossible, a dream of palaces and churches, of money and power, of dominion and decline, a paradise of beauty that was driven out of itself because the earth could not endure so much wonder.

Eternity, as is well known, is something that we are incapable really of picturing. To my way of thinking, the nearest thing to it is something like the number thousand, probably due to the round emptiness of those three noughts. A city that has been there for more than a thousand years is a tangible form of eternity. I think it is because of this that most people here seem to wander a little hesitantly, lost among all those layers of past time, that in this city all simultaneously belong to the present. In Venice anachronism lies at the very heart of things: in a thirteenth-century church you look at a fifteenth-century grave and an eighteenth-century altar; what your eyes see is what the no longer existent eyes of millions of others have seen. Here, on the contrary, that is not tragic, for while you are looking they go on talking, you are constantly accompanied by the living and the dead, you are involved in an age-old conversation. Proust, Ruskin, Rilke, Byron, Pound, Goethe, McCarthy, Morand, Brodsky, Montaigne, Casanova, Goldoni, Da Ponte, James, Montale, their words flow around you like the water in the canals, and just as the sunlight causes the waves behind the gondolas to fragment into myriad tiny sparkles, so that one word, *Venice*, echoes and sparkles in all those conversations, letters, sketches, and poems, always the same, always different. Not without reason did Paul Morand call his book about this city *Venices*, and actually even that is not enough. There ought to be a superlative degree of the plural just for this island.

I DID NOT COME over water, I came out of the sky, from one watery city to another. A man behaving like a bird, that is bound to go wrong. Then by taxi over the bridge that should never have been allowed to exist, with a driver who is in a tearing hurry, a man behaving like a hound at the hunt, it does not feel right to me, not here. But I have not come unarmed, I have the past to protect me. My luggage contains the 1906 Baedeker and the 1954 Touring Club Italiano guide. The station is still where it is supposed to be; I cannot begin to imagine how many people have arrived here by train since 1906. *"Gondeln mit einem Ruderer 1–2 fr., nachts 30 c. mehr, mit zwei Ruderern das doppelte, Gepäck jedes kleinere Stück 5 c. sind stets ausreichend vorhanden, ausserdem bis gegen Mitternacht die Stadtdampfer (Koffer und Fahrräder nicht zugelassen, Handgepäck frei). Bahnhof S. Marco 25 min. Fahrpreis 10 c. Pensionen, Riva degli Schiavoni 4133, deutsch, Zimmer von 21/2 fr. an. Möbilierte Zimmer (auch für kurze Zeit) Frau Schmütz-Monti, Sottoportico Calle dei Preti 1263. Hotel: H. Royal Danieli, nahe dem Dogenpalast, mit Aufzug, 220 z. von 5 fr. an mit Zentralheizung."* In 1954, if you took a gondola from Stazione Ferroviaria to the Alberghi del centro it cost 1,500 lire for two people, with a maximum of four suitcases; thereafter prices adapted themselves to reflect the astronomic numbers traveling by air. At the beginning of the twentieth century Louis Couperus could still travel to Venice with ten suitcases, surrounded by a throng of porters, but progress has turned us into our own servants, which is why I am lugging my two unwieldy suitcases between the masses of legs on to the *vaporetto* for a sum which, in the days of Rilke and Thomas Mann, a family could have lived on for a week. Half an hour later I am housed on the summit of an alp of four marble staircases, down an alley where you have to keep your elbows tucked in, but through six small windows I look out on to the intersection of two canals that, as an Amsterdamer, I would call *"grachten."* Just as I am opening one of the windows, a gondola containing eight frozen Japanese girls passes by with the gondolier singing *"O sole mio."* I am in Venice.

QUARTER OF AN hour, half an hour, hour, the bronze voices of time that you no longer hear in other cities, here they catch you unawares down alleyways and on bridges, as if time itself is pursuing you to tell you which piece has been struck off it now. You are lost in the labyrinth, you are looking for Santa Maria dei Miracoli, which Ezra Pound called "a jewel box," you know you are nearby, the name of the alley in which you find yourself is not listed on the map even though it is a detailed one, a bell chimes, but you do not know whether it is the one you are seeking, and then another one chimes, and yet another, and that one is no longer concerned with time, it is proclaiming something about death, cold, Cimmerian chimes, or about a wedding, or a High Mass, and then the bells break into a gallop as if they are having a race. At midday the angelus. I still know the Latin words from my schooldays: *Angelus domini nunciavit Mariae*—the angel of the Lord brought tidings to Mary—and at the same moment there they are before your very eyes, all those Annunciations in the Accademia, in the Ca' d'Oro, in the churches, those by Lorenzo Veneziano, and those by the Bellinis, Byzantine and Gothic, always the same wingéd man and the Virgin, you see them so often that you are no longer surprised that a man has wings, no more than you are surprised by all the other fantasy figures, crowned lions, unicorns, people who fly through the air, griffins, dragons, they simply belong here. You are the one who is lost in the territory of the dream, the fable, the fairy tale, and if you are sensible you will let yourself be lost. You were looking for something, a palace, the house of a poet, but you lose your way, you turn down an alleyway that ends in a wall or on an embankment without a bridge, and suddenly you realize that this is what it is all about, that only now are you seeing the things that you would never have seen otherwise. You stand still, and what you hear are footsteps, the forgotten sound that belongs to an age without cars, that has rung out here uninterrupted throughout the centuries. Shuffling, vehement, hurried, slow, sauntering steps, an orchestra with instruments of leather, rubber, wood, sandals, high heels, boots, sneakers, yet always stirring to human time, swelling to a crescendo in the hours of daylight, then gradually dying away as it grows dark, until all you hear are solos, and finally the solitary aria of your own feet reverberating in the narrow dark alley, on the marble stairs, and then there is only silence, until it is time for the city to say one last thing: that midnight arrives even in fables. Looking out from my high windows, in the all-encompassing silence I hear the Marangona, the great bell of the Campanile being rung one last time, muffled, heavy, commanding chimes. The city on the water is closing, this is the end of all the stories . . . go to sleep. No more movement on the motionless water below, no voices, no footsteps. The doge is asleep, Tintoretto is asleep, Monteverdi is asleep, Rilke is asleep, Goethe is asleep, the lions, dragons, basilicas, the statues of saints and heroes, they all sleep, until the first ships with fish and fresh vegetables put in to port and the symphony of a hundred thousand feet begins once more.

ZINC LIGHT, the painter does not yet know what he is going to do with this day, leave it as it is, add some more copper, a greenish sheen, accentuate the gray, or alternatively flood everything with more light. Nice weather for bats; when it starts to rain everybody puts up their umbrellas, everybody changes into their own bat. Five minutes later the sun has come out again, the wind is blowing across the Riva degli Schiavoni, the water is as ruffled as a nervous actress, I am sitting on some small wooden steps that stick some way out into the water, and I can smell the sea at my feet. Petrarch lived here, it says on the wall behind me, *l'illustre messer Francesco Petrarca essendogli compagno nell'incantavole soggiorno l'amico Giovanni Boccaccio*, and now I want to see what they saw when they stood in front of the house, these two masters with their contemplative eyes. The point at the far end of the sestiere Dorsoduro, where now two Atlases shoulder the golden globe on the tower of the Dogana, but that was not there then. In those days it was called Punta del Sale, because of the many salt depots on Le Zattere. And right opposite, the small island where the formidable neoclassicism of San Giorgio Maggiore now stands was home to a Benedictine abbey, which if Petrarch and Boccaccio were now standing next to me, would puzzlingly have disappeared. How would I explain that to them, Palladio? The nostalgia for the pure lines of pre-Christian Rome that built these enormous triumphal temples on top of their humble, probably pre-Roman, probably brick abbey dating from 982, just as that same heathen nostalgia built the equally proud Redentore, a few meters further along La Giudecca, and the Salute just beyond the Dogana near the Canal Grande. Only San Marco would be recognized by the two masters, or at least the shape of it; the rest would be a vision, something that in a mysterious way simultaneously resembled an imaginable past and an unimaginable future. But once again these are the dreams of anachronism, and this time they are forbidden dreams, for while I am sitting there lost in my musings, I watch how a small police launch skirts around me, turning and returning, manoeuvring in the way that only water-born Venetians can. The *carabiniere* sticks his head out of the window and tells me I am not allowed to sit there: I am four meters too far off the coast on my coconut mat, this is a *zona militare*. I get up obediently. I can hardly explain that I am having a conversation with Petrarch and Boccaccio, and one does not jest with the maritime power of La Serenissima, you can check that in every port on the coast!

IT IS BOUND to happen. You have been wandering in the Accademia all day, you have seen a solid mile of painted canvas, it is the fourth, the sixth, or the eighth day and you feel as though you are swimming against a powerful current of gods, kings, prophets, martyrs, monks, virgins, and monsters; that Ovid, Hesiod, the Old and New Testament have accompanied you the whole way, that you are being pursued by the *Lives of the Saints* and Christian and heathen iconography, that Catherine's wheel, Sebastian's arrows, Hermes' wingéd sandals, Mars's helmet, and all lions of stone, gold, porphyry, and marble are out to get you. Frescos, tapestries, gravestones, everything is charged with meaning, refers to real or imaginary events; armies of sea-gods, putti, popes, sultans, *condottieri*, admirals, all clamour for your attention. They whoosh by along the ceilings, look down at you with their painted, woven, sketched, and sculpted eyes. Sometimes you see the same saint more than once in one day, in a Gothic, Byzantine, baroque, or classical disguise, for myths are mighty and the heroes are adaptable, Renaissance or rococo, it does not bother them, as long as you keep looking, as long as their essence remains intact. Once they were employed to convey the power of their masters, in an age when everyone knew what they depicted; Virtue, Death, or Daybreak, War, Revelation, Liberty, they played their part in the allegories assigned to them, they commemorated confessors and church fathers, generals and bankers; nowadays different sorts of armies pass by, those of the tourists who no longer understand their visual language, no longer know what they signify or used to signify; only their beauty has remained, the genius of the master who made them, so there they stand, a nation of Stone Guests, waving from the façades of churches, leaning out of the *trompe-l'oeils* of the *palazzi*, the *ragazzi* of Tiepolo and Fumiani race around up there, and once again St. Julian is beheaded, once again the Madonna cradles her baby, once again Perseus battles with Medusa, Alexander converses with Diogenes. The traveler draws back from all the tumult, for the moment he wants no more, just to sit on a stone seat on the embankment, and watch how a Slavonian grebe searches for its prey in the brackish, greenish water, watch the movement of the water itself, pinch himself in the arm to reassure himself that he is not sculpted or painted. Could it be, he thinks, that there are more madonnas in Venice than living women? Does anyone actually know how many painted, sculpted, ivory-carved, silver-embossed Venetians there are? And just imagine, he thinks, but that is only because he is so tired, if they all rose up together, left their frames, niches, predellas, plinths, tapestries, cornices, to drive the Japanese, the Americans, the Germans from their gondolas, occupy the restaurants and finally, with their swords and shields, their purple cloaks and crowns, tridents and wings, demand payment for ten centuries of loyal service?

A DAY OF SMALL things. Despite the wind and the cold I sit on the fo'c's'le of the *vaporetto*, lashed by the rain, having jumped on deck from the jetty and back on to the jetty from the deck, wanting to be ferried like this every day, with the moving element of the water all about you; the promise of travel. Once, in 1177, here on the forecourt of San Marco, the powerful Venetians forced Barbarossa to kiss the foot of Pope Alexander III and afterward, outside on the piazza, to help His Holiness into the stirrups of the papal donkey. To show his gratitude, the Pope had given the doge a ring with which each year, on Ascension Day, he could wed the sea: "We wed thee, Sea, as a mark of true and eternal dominion." The sea was subsequently on many occasions unfaithful to her repeatedly new but still identical husband, but she remained true in one respect: every morning the stone tables of the fish market are laden with silver treasure, *orata* and *spigolo*, *capone* and *sostiola*, and all the other colors, the sepia that is stained with ink, as if the writer could not find the right word, the still living, writhing *anguilla*, red with blood from the gashes made by the chopping knife, the crab who, with his eight claws, is still searching for life, the living stones of mussels, oysters, cockles—anyone from the Middle Ages would recognize them, just as he would recognize the *Pescaria* that has been here, by the Rialto Bridge on the Canal Grande, for more than a thousand years, next to the oldest church in Venice, San Giacometto. I have gone inside under the clock, which is much too big, with its single hand and twenty-four massive Roman numerals, past the five slender columns with their Corinthian capitals that have looked out on fish and vegetables since 900.

If I understand my guide correctly, everything in here has been rebuilt and altered, but now is not the time to get involved with art history. An elderly priest in a green chasuble blesses his parishioners and is about to say something. The church is full; it looks like a living room where the guests have kept their coats on. They are among friends, they know one another, it is as though they are aware that there has been praying on this spot for 1,500 years, as though they themselves have stood at the deathbed of the Roman gods, just as they have also heard, from beyond, the peculiar uproar of the Reformation and the French Revolution, the screams coming from the Sportpalast and the clanking of the Iron Curtain. Here, in the meantime, nothing had changed. Somebody who, later on, in Turin, embraced a carthorse had apparently claimed that God was dead, but they had still continued to address him in the same words they had always used, and now the old man shuffled up to the altar of St. Anthony and held aloft a holy relic; a bone or a bit of monk's habit behind glass, I could not see which. The priest asks the great saint of the wilderness to be with us in our *debolezza*. When I look up the word later, just to make sure, I see that it says "weakness," not a bad definition at all. Afterward the men stay and talk for a while under the six sanctuary lamps, in which burning oil wicks glow behind panes of red glass. The priest departs, a far too thin plastic jacket draped over his cassock, everyone shakes hands. I have a quick look at the confessional. A shabby mauve curtain hangs in front; the confessor has no chance of concealing himself. Whoever whispers his sins here may as well have them broadcast. The walls whisper old messages about the oil decanters' guild (*travasadori d'olio*), the corn sieve makers' guild, and the carriers' guild, about the doge who came here each Thursday before Easter throughout the centuries to honour the saint, but I have an appointment with the greatest of all the Venetian painters in the Scuola di San Giorgio degli Schiavoni, Vittore Carpaccio.

In the Accademia he has his own room where you are caught up in his universe when, on all four walls, he relates the legend of St. Ursula, a series of paintings that one should write a book about. Here in the Scuola it is no less magnificent, but today I have come back to this small, intimate space to see a single painting, the vision of the greatest saint among writers and the greatest writer among saints, Augustine of Hippo. Perhaps I have done so because it shows a writer's study, in which I would like immediately to take up residence. True, I could not presume upon the mitre on the altar, the staff, or the statue of Christ with cross and banner, but the perfect light, the open books, the score, the shell, which appears to be a *Cypraea tigris*, the beautiful, bound folios against the left-hand wall, perhaps containing manuscripts, the revolving bookcase, the intriguing letter lying somewhere in the middle of the floor, and the small fluffy dog with his two paws planted in front of him, his nose in the air and those two bright, cherry-black eyes, no, whoever cannot write here will not be able to write anywhere. The saint himself is captured at that most mysterious of moments: inspiration. He holds his pen in the air, the light pours in, he hears how the words form themselves and is almost sure of how he will write them down, one second later, when Carpaccio has left, he dips his pen in the sepia ink and writes the sentence that is now preserved in all the libraries of the world, in one of his books.

THE END. A last day that in another year will be a first one again, for between Venice and Venice much may be forgotten. I am going to visit the dead. From the Fondamente Nove I take the *vaporetto* that goes to the island of death, San Michele, and then on to Murano. In a splendid novella by Alejo Carpentier, *Concierto Barocco*, there is a scene in which, after a night of wild partying, full of music and wine, Handel and Vivaldi, the red-haired Venetian priest, go with a few others to the island to have breakfast. They drink and chew, while Vivaldi, munching on a piece of hog's head marinated in vinegar, marjoram and paprika, walked off a few paces, only to stop suddenly in front of a nearby grave at which he had been gazing for some considerable time because it displayed a name that was unprecedentedly melodious for these parts. He spelled out "IGOR STRAVINSKY."

"Oh, that's right," Handel said, spelling out the letters in turn, "he wanted to be buried in this cemetery."

"A creditable musician," Antonio said, "but sometimes his ideas were very old-fashioned. He was inspired by the traditional themes: Apollo, Orpheus, Persephone . . . how much longer?"

"I know his *Oedipus Rex*," Handel said. "Some people think that the end of the first act (*"Gloria, gloria, gloria, Oedipus uxor"*) is reminiscent of my music."

"But . . . whatever possessed him to write a profane cantata based on a Latin text?" Antonio said.

"His *Canticum Sacrum* has also been performed, in San Marco," George Frederick said. "It contains melismas in the sort of medieval style that we have long since rejected."

"Yes, the so-called avant-garde masters do try terribly hard to work out how past composers did things . . . sometimes they even try to modernize their style. In that respect we are more modern. I don't give a fig what the operas or concerts of a hundred years ago were like. I follow my own path, to the best of my own unique ability and insight, and that's that."

"I feel just the same," Handel said, ". . . although you do have to take account of the fact that—"

"Oh, do stop talking such balls for once," Filomeno said and tipped wine down his throat from the bottle he had just uncorked. And the four of them reached into the hampers from the Ospedale della Pietà again, hampers that, just like the mythological horns of plenty, never seemed to run out. So that by the time they got to the quince cheese and the honey cake, the last of the morning clouds had parted and the sun shone directly upon the gravestones that now lay like brilliant white slabs beneath the deep green of the cypresses. It was surely due to the fullness of the light, that the Russian name, so close by, caught their attention once more.

It is almost closing time when I arrive at the cemetery. I walk past the gatekeeper, am given a map of the dead with the abodes of Stravinsky, Diaghilev, Ezra Pound, and the freshly typed-in Joseph Brodsky. It is unfitting; everyone is asleep and I am practically hurrying. I pass by the children's graves: marble structures for souls that lived for a few days only, and portraits of boys in whose eyes you can still discern the invisible football. I cross the dividing line between the *militari del Mare* and *della Terra*, as if those sorts of distinctions still matter where they have gone, and arrive in due course at the evangelical section; palms, cypresses, truncated columns, mossy pyramids, the nineteenth-century grammar of death. Most of the graves themselves have expired, the inscriptions illegible, Danes, Germans, consuls, nobility, and in between all that, the two horizontal stones of Olga Rudge and Ezra Pound, enclosed within a low, heart-shaped border of plants. Not much further on, a little hill of almost sandy-colored earth with a few bunches of wilted, withered flowers and a thin, rude, white, wooden cross with pebbles on the arms, Joseph Brodsky. In the *reparto Greco* behind the wall, among Russian princes and Greek poets, lie Igor and Vera Stravinsky. Handel and Vivaldi have just left, but they have left their flowers behind, on each of the graves lie a pink rose and a blue iris, laid crossways. I think how many years ago it is that, in New York, I asked Vera Stravinsky whether at the end of his life, when he was more than eighty, Stravinsky did not find the repeated trips to Venice tiring, whereupon she exclaimed in that glorious Russian accent: "Ach, you don't understand! Stravinsky, he LOVVED THE FLYINK!"

A mechanical voice from the land of the dead reverberates across the island, a herald as polyglot as the Pope. In German, English, Russian, and Japanese we are requested to leave the dead in peace, the gates are closing. Hurry, *ragazzi*, hurry, cry the gravediggers, whose practiced ears have heard the *vaporetto* approaching, and so we all rush to the jetty, as if someone with a scythe is in pursuit. When we reach open water I can see Murano on one side and Venice on the other. The orange lights indicating the channel have come on, the two islands float like shades, one big and one small, on the dark water and then all of a sudden, from behind a black cloud, comes a coppery shaft of sunset which for a few seconds long envelops the city in front of me in an apocalyptic blaze, as if that dream down below has gone on long enough.

1998

Lady Wright *and* Sir Jawara:
a Boat Trip up the Gambia

To avoid any confusion: The Gambia is a country, called after the river of the same name. It is in Africa, which contains a great many other countries that not a soul has ever heard of, or knows the whereabouts of. *This* country that no one has ever heard of forms a strange, English-speaking enclave in the southern part of French-speaking Senegal, and consists of an extremely wide river, with, as you would expect, two river banks. Upon these banks, and sometimes on the river as well, the population of Gambia lives, 400,000 of them, about the same as the population of Surinam* would have been, were it not slowly draining away. It is hot there, and its people make a living by cultivating peanuts. In addition, it is independent (as far as that is possible in this world), has no standing army, which is very rare, no television, which is extremely restful, only one newspaper, which appears thrice weekly, and a parliament that convenes once every two months, thereby making it a democracy. Foreign papers are only available in a thoroughly yellowed state, the radio broadcasts in Wolof, Mandinke, Fulani, and, it is said, in English as well—so anyone wishing to bid the world a temporary farewell knows where to go. There are roads, of which two hundred kilometers are tarmac, but no newspaper

---

* Translator's note: the former Dutch colony in the Caribbean had just gained its independence and a sizable number of its population were immigrating to the Netherlands.

kiosks, and outside the capital, which is on the coast, no hotels either. There are four Gambian pounds to one British pound, although a Gambian pound is also called a dalasi, and contains a hundred bututs. I am back home now, and have fallen prey to a certain nostalgia. "Why did you go there?" my friends ask, once they have grasped where it is I have been, but that is just it, I did not *go* there at all, I merely arrived there. I intended to go to the Spanish Sahara. "Intended" in the sense in which Nijhoff uses it in his poem "The Child and I": "I would fishing go . . ." So I had had every intention of going to the Sahara; the safe-conduct pass, required by the military authorities on the spot, was supposed to be waiting for me at the ministry in Madrid. Only it was not, and what is more, it would not be arriving in the near future. March in Madrid is cold and inclement. So what now?

The reason I had wanted to go to the Spanish Sahara in the first place had to do with the fact that Mauritania was laying claim to the area. At the embassy in Brussels, in order to obtain a Mauritanian visa, I had had to listen to hours of enthusing about Rembrandt's use of light, delivered by an exceptionally snazzy dresser, an entirely artificial-looking Mauritanian, who, by the sound of him, was no Einstein. He asked me to consider for a moment, if I would, the great *African* King Tutankhamun. Could I visualize him?

"Yes? The noble features? The truly royal expression? Exactly! And just compare that to your great king, who *also* referred to himself as the Sun King. Louis XIV, yes, exactly! But he, Mr. Nooteboom, *he* was in the habit of pissing behind the sofas in Versailles . . . the Trianon still stinks of it!"

Neither would he grant me a visa, despite "Rambran's" use of light, because according to him my passport was "too full."

I said this smacked of bureaucratic pettiness, to which he replied that they had learned that from us. But when, the following morning, I returned to the Islamic republic's embassy, armed with a new passport hot from the presses of the Dutch embassy, and as empty as a cot prior to the birth of the first child, I still did not get my visa. I protested till I was blue in face and finally left empty-handed.

It is starting to rain in Madrid. The Sahara does not want me, Mauritania does not want me, and it is cold here. On my ticket it says "via Las Palmas." I glance at the map of the world hanging conveniently in the window of British Overseas Airways. Next to me, a vendor selling lottery tickets cries out that this is my last chance. That is just how I feel too. The best decisions are made at five to six Dutch time, and in Spain at five to eight (when the shops close). A huge longing for Africa has welled up in me. Is there a flight tomorrow from Las Palmas to Dakar? (An excellent jumping-off point, Dakar was my first experience of Africa. Nostalgia!) Yes, sir, there are two flights to Dakar, but they are both full.

Through my tears, I catch sight of another name on that big map, just below Dakar. Bathurst! Bathurst? "Are there any flights to Bathurst?" "Nowadays it's called Banjul, sir." "Oh. And are there any flights to Banjul?" "Yes, sir, with British Columbian, departing from Las Palmas, once a week, and it's tomorrow." Fate strikes again. Over the telephone (it is now one minute before eight) she organizes a new episode in my life. Without her I would never have read the *Gambian News Bulletin*, never have eaten peppered oysters, never have met Mr. Dembo, and I would never have been arrested in a temperature of forty degrees centigrade, for failing to dismount from my bicycle briskly enough when Sir Dawda Jawara passed by. And I have not even mentioned the *Lady Wright*.

But it is still cold, dark, and Europe. Yet less than twenty-four hours later, an airplane is winging its way high above the forbidden, scorched Sahara, with me in it. It loses height along the

African coast, until it reaches a spot where wide rivers wend their way through limitless flats, which is where we make our descent, together with the encroaching blackness of night. The airport lights appear to be flickering strangely, and once we have landed I can see why. They consist of bottles of tallow, giving off bluish flames. Welcome.

Trees, the priestly shadows of baobabs, a small group of black people by a gate, a fire engine that races along beside us, the scrubbed-white Scottish stewardesses, already quite out of place here, the manufactured air inside the plane, which I shall shortly be exchanging for the lukewarm air of a tropical night. I realize how little I know about the Gambia, except that Queen Victoria, who never came here, regarded it as "such a darling little place," and that according to my neighbor, who has never set foot here either, there is only one hotel in the capital that "you can go to." So that is where I go. After the passport brawl and the luggage brawl, I set off for Banjul in a light blue Renault 4. Alternate gusts of hot and cold air fill the car—evenings on the coast, I learn later, can be extremely cool. It is dark already; I can see small fires, people gathered around them, black clumps of trees hewn out of the black night, nothing more. This morning at six I was still in Madrid and I realize that none of my friends or relations knows I am at this extraordinary spot, and feel rather elated. There is a lot to be said for a touch of "non-being." Reclining in a taxi, like a fatigued gentleman, in a country where no one knows anything about you, is like acting a part. You are filling in for somebody else at the last minute and do not yet know the script. The driver immediately attempts to alter it. He thinks I should go to the Apollo Hotel, not the recommended Atlantic. It is far more reasonable. I have visions of cockroaches, mosquitoes, and sleepless nights, and tell him I want to go to the Atlantic. "Apollo, small price," he says. "Many white people"—he knows his onions. But I assume he has some sort of arrangement with the Apollo, and stick to my guns. Of course on the following day I move to the Apollo, something he never failed to rib me about whenever we met, which was often, because in Banjul you keep coming across the same taxi drivers.

The extremely black man at the reception desk is positively frosty. Yes, there are still rooms available. When I remark that it does seem rather expensive ("Don't you have a slightly cheaper room?"), he advises me that there is always the Apollo. But by now I am determined to sleep here. While he is laboriously copying down my passport details, I see a stenciled sheet of paper in a wooden display case: *The Progressive Newspaper*, no. 664 (WE PURSUE THE TRUTH, published twice weekly, price thirteen bututs). I make my first Gambian purchase, and a short while later am sitting, surrounded by the bare stone walls of my stony room, listening to the monotonous ballad of the air conditioning, and reading a rousing protest about "our South Korean friends" not having been invited to attend the march past on Independence Day, which "flies in the face of all the rules of etiquette on such a historic occasion." *Verbum sat sapienti*, the article concludes meaningfully, and although I am not sure whether many readers will understand it, one thing is clear: I am still very much part of the human race. Forever finding fault with one another, no matter where you go.

I wash off the dust of three countries and go outside. It rustles and smells sweet, a bit squelchy, boggy. To the left of me lies the river, which is miles wide at this point. Not a light to be seen. Walking, looking. Marine Parade. Government House, a white colonial ghost. The two black guards signal to me that I cannot just swan by in front of it, but should use the path of loose sand closer to the river. The tennis club, the Albert market, Nigerian Airways, Mahoney's Cinema—a John Wayne film showing. And why not? Buckle Street, Orange Street, Lemon Street.

I can hear my shoes on the tarmac, among the shuffling of

slippers, the lisping of sandals, and the soft flapping sound of bare feet. Occasional groups of men squat at the sandy edge of the street, playing huge games of backgammon and draughts. They sit and lounge in the dim light, their lips murmuring a strange language which shuts me out, making me even more of a foreigner. "Hey, friend!" a boy calls, and waves back when I wave. It is all extremely quiet and extremely peaceful. Now and then a puddle of neon light affords a somewhat better view. H.R. Carrol & Co., Shyben A. Madi & Sons, mysterious shops full of cloth and suitcases, but in most places the yellowish light has a fuzzy and blurry effect, which fits in with my mood perfectly. Tomorrow it will all acquire a face. Through ever darker streets I find my way with difficulty back to the hotel. In the shower my forty-one-year-old body performs a death-defying backwards somersault over something slippery, and comes to rest across the raised stony edge of the basin. No blood, nothing broken. So it is no coincidence, I am indeed here for a purpose. I read a poem by Tibullus ("Do not hurt me, Goddess, I have done nothing to deserve it") and go to bed. Outside I hear a call I never normally hear, and on it I sail away.

Coffee, sugar crumbs, crumbly bread, bougainvillea, frangipane, hibiscus, flirting acacias above the terrace, the green brilliance of the river, this is how the day begins. What on earth have I done now? I am here without a mission, having been assigned here solely by me. But what does "being somewhere" mean? The same as always, only somewhere else, and with all the cameras and tape recorders open, on and wired up to that empty storehouse where sounds and images are converted into memories.

But it is vital to introduce some method into this luxury. Of course it is wonderful to saunter along the capital's few furnace-hot streets, savoring sensual experiences, but by the end of it one is left with little more than a residue of subjective feelings and the conjecture which goes with them. No, a method. Such as, for instance: Foreign Correspondent Wishes to Interview President. True, one can doubt the immediate practical use of this—nobody in Holland is going to lose any sleep over an interview with an unknown president of an unknown country.

And yet, the long trek up the rickety staircase of a bureaucratic machine can produce unexpected insights, so long as you do not start at the top. So on that Friday morning I take my first steps toward a president who, in the end, I do not manage to reach, but that was not the point anyway: the secret objective is the shadow-play along the way. In order for this method to succeed, however, there is one precondition: you have passionately to want to meet the president, otherwise the torments along the way will not yield the desired return.

THE ONLY FOREIGN tourists who come to Gambia are Swedes. Twenty kilometers from the capital, along the wild ocean coast, an enterprising Swede has built three low-rise hotels into which, each week, an aeroplane full of Swedes is emptied. They fly eight hours for the privilege, paying little more than £300, for two weeks' travel and board, and the consequences for Gambia have been significant. To the utter chagrin of the English colonial types, who have often been in Africa for a quarter of a century or more, all palefaces are now unfailingly addressed in Swedish: "*Hey du Svenska!*" And, in addition, the ladies among the Swedes, who form the majority as it is, show a marked preference for a somewhat deeper contact with the many young Gambians who flutter in and around the hotels. This promotes fraternal relations, if not indeed maternal ones, but the local guardians of the community's morals regard it as a great decline. For the boys involved it provides a handy way of supplementing their income, and easy access to the nightclubs belonging to the hotels. And so the big wide world has come to Gambia, and not everyone is pleased about it, or as the taxi driver put it: "Him no good. Gambia girl no go with him. She know his family. Is no good. Swedish girl she do not know. She come she go."

A small tourist bazaar has also been set up especially for the Swedes, where colorful dyed cloth, shirts, and hats are displayed for sale. In among all the happily flapping garments stands a kiosk containing an attractive, languid woman, who is in charge of "Information." I buy a map of the town and one of the country, plus a book about ten years of independence, as well as the national anthem ("For the Gambia, our homeland / We strive and work and pray / That all may live in unity, / Freedom and peace each day") and a book on birds. But she cannot help me with the president, I need the ministry for that, on McCarthy Square. It is not far, but as the day progresses it seems to be getting hotter by the minute. Shade only means not having the sun burning your face, but the burden of hot, wet towels around your shoulders grows steadily heavier. A large crowd is sitting on the steps of the ministry. They are hawking plastic birds, cigarettes, cola nuts, peanuts and tiny, sour oranges, and all call out *"Hey du Svenska!"* The mood is good-natured. The square itself is a green sea of English grass, a huge cricket pitch surrounded by wooden, colonial buildings. Half close your eyes, traveler, and you are back in the days of yore—the cricketers fan out across the pitch, it is 1920, 1910, 1890, some of the uniforms alter occasionally, a few more white faces arrive, but apart from that nothing changes: the Wolof, Malinke, Fulani, and Soninke are still recognizably themselves, the times may perhaps have changed, the plume on the governor's cocked hat has disappeared, but the heat, the river, the tribes, and the poverty remain. Independent heat, independent river, independent poverty.

Past two black Mercedes sporting flags, and a policeman with black knees above dark blue woollen socks, I come to a reception desk. At which desk would you have to apply in Holland, in order to speak to the Queen? While I stand there in the sunlight debating this, someone beckons me inside. The place is a shambles, that much is obvious. I recognize it immediately for it resembles my own study. Nothing filed away properly, the newspapers in disorder, no proper cabinets, impossible to find things, running out of everything, on top of one another and muddled up together, letters, forms, on chairs, tables, and floor. Three people sit there working—that is what I always call it too. One of them is searching fruitlessly among a pile of old letters. A young woman, whose beauty I find positively riveting, speaks into the telephone in a high-pitched sing-song voice, undoubtedly to a lover concealed within it. Nothing else happens for the time being. I shove a few newspapers aside ("Peking lends Gambia 28 million dalasis") and settle down to await events. The fan attached to the ceiling whirls loose sheets of paper about, people come in, look me up and down as if debating whether or not to purchase me, and disappear again without having undertaken anything. Gradually the same old feeling begins to take hold, that this is not really happening. I am not sitting here at all. It is a play by an African Pinter, for which I have been engaged at a huge sum. Shortly, it will be time for the interval, then we will all rise, gauge the applause and go and have a beer in the canteen.

Not true, any of it. From behind the farthest desk, someone awakes from a deep reverie, makes a swift alteration to the theory of relativity lying in front of him, and walks gracefully toward me.

What exactly do I want?

"To interview the president."

I might as well have said that I had come to see the manuscript of Beethoven's Ninth.

"Oh, I see. Then you must speak to Mr. N'Jie."

But Mr. N'Jie is not around. Mr. N'Jie and I are locked in some sort of weird capillary action: as soon as I am poured into an office he bubbles up . . . and out. And so begins a wondrous charade of meetings, appointments, waitings in the corridor, then another corridor, still more gentlemen, some of whom are also called N'Jie. Meanwhile, I collect stencils and do my homework. If there had been anything the slightest bit tragic about it, I could start citing Kafka—gent lost in maze of offices, etc.—but there is not; it is simply the long-drawn-out beginning of a film without a plot. I drift from office to office, depositing the occasional banknote with discretion, listening to great dreams, learning who comes from which tribe, and that they themselves often cannot tell just from looking at one another, hand over a list of questions in English for His Excellency, and scramble in this fashion across the Gambian snakes and ladders board, back and forth, up and down. It is most educational. I have gradually forgotten the outside world; all that remain are the hot, dusty streets, the dining room of the Apollo Hotel, and my tiny stone room that affords me a view of the river, along which peanut boats from the far interior putter, under three-cornered sails. At certain times of the day there comes the faintly pestilential reek of the open sewer, and every morning I wake up extremely early, when the first people arrive to draw water from the well beneath my window.

The newspapers at the British Council are more than a month old, and the only book about the Gambia that I have been able to find in the undernourished bookshop is the *Official Handbook of the Gambian Colony and Protectorate,* published in 1906. It is all there. Every name, every amount, every procedure, everyone's salary, everything. Under the heading Letter Boxes: "There are no letter boxes in the colony and the Protectorate." It makes incredible reading. So this is how an empire is run. Nothing has been left to chance. Someone, once, worked it all out. A telegram from Bathurst to St. Helena costs three shillings. Jeremiah Collingwood, sergeant major in the military police, "accompanied Sir Alfred Maloney, Sir James Shaw Hay and Sir Gilbert Carter on several missions in the hinterland"; he is twenty-seven years of age, has been in the colony for five months, and earns £100 a year. In 1903 government ships earned £366, 1s and 6d less than was expected. A letter to Wei-Hai-Wei, the Cayman Islands and Fiji cost 1d, and reports on any floggings meted out should be submitted ultimately to the Admiralty, in duplicate. Wholly bygone time, 364 pages of it, all of it true. Reading a book like this, you are torn between hilarity and melancholy and vice versa, but when you glance outside at the shabby town, lying in a sort of kink in the enormous river, when you think of the single tarmac road and the lack of roughly everything, you have to ask yourself just what the English got up to during all that time. And the answer would have to be: not much really; peanuts!

The foreign secretary of Sierra Leone has arrived, and the governor of the Central Bank is attending a meeting of the West African Sub-Regional Commission of the Association of African Central Banks in Lagos. Today Kabba Jatta from Sutokoba has been dismissed as Head of the Wuii District, at the Roxy they are showing *Le Shériff* with Virginia Mayo, and the sun will be setting, just like yesterday and tomorrow, at 7:17 PM. I have dined at table 13 again, have cycled on my rented bike along the narrow path between the mangrove swamps to the coast, have swum in the ocean, jotted down the names of three trees (neem, casurina, and *keseng-keseng*), and was back at the harbor in time to watch the hundreds of crows flying home to roost in the stripped-bare old tree, as they do every evening. A few people are standing looking at a strangely dilapidated white riverboat. She is called the *Lady Wright*, and dips backwards at a slightly crazy angle, her paint is peeling and she bears a passing resemblance to Humphrey Bogart's *African Queen*. A dignified old black man with streaks of tinselly gray in his hair calls down to me from the rail.

"You want to come on de ship?"

"Where does she go?"

"Up de rivvah! To Bassé!"

Back at the hotel I look at the map. The river snakes far into the African interior. Bassé lies at the back door of Gambia, approximately four hundred kilometres from Banjul.

"Very, very hot," Mr. N'Jie says pityingly, when I explain my new hankering to him. But it is a whole lot easier than reaching the president. For you can purchase it. The following afternoon we go together to the Ports Authority. *This* Mr. N'Jie is uncommonly tall and possessed of sharp, aristocratic features. He has just returned from an official visit to Dakar. Compared to Dakar—a turbulent, sophisticated, incredibly expensive Mediterranean city full of international tourism—Banjul is Barnstaple. But Mr. N'Jie does not think much of it. "They have lost their African character. They are like copies of the French." The worst fear of English-speaking Gambians is that they will be swallowed up by the French-speaking Senegalese. Mr. N'jie is a Wolof, and I ask him whether he speaks Wolof when he meets a fellow Wolof at the Senegalese Ministry. Granted, yes, but only because the Senegalese are too stuck up to speak English. Europe has certainly left its imprint.

The riverboat will be leaving in a day's time. Providing the engines hold up, she does the trip in three to four days. My return

journey will be arranged by the president of the Transport Union,
Mr. Daddy Soul, and by the time I get back "things" are bound to
have been straightened out with that other president. Daddy Soul
requires payment in advance, a not negligible sum, but it will entitle
me to be brought back from Bassé to Banjul by Peugeot, and I can
stop wherever I want to. Talking through this momentous agree-
ment takes one hour, but by the end I do have the backing of an
entire union. "You must purchase something for dee mosquitoes,"
Daddy Soul says, shaking my hand at length. "And you must take
de medi-cin. Ah, and it will be very, very hot." I am beginning to
believe it.

The next day, the chief problem is getting on board. The riverboat itself has become invisible beneath a pyramid of human
bodies interlaced with baggage. There is no boarding plank, but
next to the wheelhouse, like a beacon, stands the silver-haired

black man who extended such a friendly invitation to me a few days ago. He indicates to me how to get on board, with a hop, spring and a jump. I wrestle my way through the shouting, sweating, but good-humoured throng, past baskets of salted fish, mattresses, chests of salt, mounds of earthenware, children, sailors, nut vendors, sacking, woodwork, bicycles, and a cat, up the exceedingly narrow stairs to the first-class deck. Mr. Dembo is waiting for me there, the sun shining on his sparkly hair. He is the chief steward, and he shows me my hut, which is about the same size as I am. The sheets are gray and heavily stained. "Dey are clean sheets," Mr. Dembo says with satisfaction, and who am I to contradict him? A wistful horn is sounding on the wooden pier, and suddenly I feel the boat lurch, violently, as if everybody wants to get on or off at the same time. When I go outside I see that this is indeed the case: everybody *is* trying to get on or off at the same time. We are listing. A section of the random pile of crates, baskets, and sacks begins to slide. Panic. An entire marriage bed lands on someone's head. Up on deck, a small group of abandoned whites stand watching it all. More and more people come running from all directions, women in the most beautiful garments, draped with bunches of children, bearers with cargo for which there cannot possibly be room, but forget it, there is still room for more . . . and yet more.

A mysterious messenger from the underworld approaches, wings of dust on his sculpted feet. He is waving a handful of slips of pink paper. The crowd parts, and he whirls on to the boat. The captain examines the papers and gives a sign. Three blasts on the ship's hooter. Deep within the boat, the engines heave a deep sigh. We start to shake. Everyone who is not coming springs ashore.

"Head slow starboard! Half ahead!"

"Go two ahead slow. Steady as you go. Full ahead!"

The bell sounds four times, we draw slowly away from the quayside, leaving behind the wailing, grinning, clamorous throng, which soon shrinks until it blends into the faraway river bank like a little clump of human reeds. With the last hawser, the world has been cast off too. Any ship is a limited universe with its own rules and times, and these now start to apply. Next to me, in an equally rickety deckchair, sits a Big Wheel from the interior, who, during the next few days, will continue to amaze me by the range of his mind-boggling headgear. Today he is wearing a green deerstalker and yellow mules. His head is broad, Mongolian, and decorated with a moustache fit for Pythagoras: a black triangle of which the sharply angled upper corner seems to point at his nose. His smile is as sweet as caramel and does not wane for a moment. In the crook of his arm he cradles his transistor like a tiny, rectangular child. An agent in Scout's uniform guards our deck against intruders, inefficiently, thank goodness. Gulls screech, both river banks grow veiled, it is slightly misty, I see ghostly pirogues beneath the northern bank, just like a Turner. Peace descends upon us, kilos of it—the quiet, plodding chug-chug-chug, a cup of ebony tea from Mr. Dembo, the darkness that is advancing—my soul curls itself up in its basket and is content.

Only when the bell sounds for dinner do I see my fellow passengers on this ship of fools, all assembled. They are a motley bunch. A provocatively attractive, red-haired Danish beautician. Her boyfriend, a bank clerk, and two other Danes living out a miserable existence in Greenland. One of them is so happy to be away from the place that he never stops laughing. The other one might well wish to do the same, but his face has been so parboiled by the sun that he looks like a sausage. Alcohol will unite us for the rest of the trip. Then there is Mother Denmark, a woman constructed out of enough material for three. Her gigantic personage inspires awe even in the captain, no shrimp himself. She films everything it is possible to film, and has a tape recorder for the hours of darkness. A happy soul. Three Swedes make up the Scandinavian contingent. A happy camper who does not speak a word of English and establishes an intimate contact with a young African mother, who cannot be more than fourteen. An airy-fairy woman from the North, who has been everywhere, and has come across great dollops of magic and mysticism everywhere too, about which she preaches in an accent like Ingrid Bergman's in *Murder on the Orient Express* ("Zose Zings can not be ezplained. You zee ze needul go zru ze handt and come out at ze ozze zide. No blud. No paiyn. It is madgik"), and an elderly, obese Viking, who says nothing the whole journey and reads detective stories.

Also at my table is an American in the Peace Corps, a young girl who will spend the next two years far from everything, in a village on the river, setting up a laboratory. She is accompanied by a Gambian who has been allotted the task of teaching her Mandinke. Endearingly serious, she studies without pause. Later on, when we have all returned, she will remain, cooped up in that baking cauldron of a village. Then, even Banjul, far off and inaccessible, will seem like an inviting town. According to Corps rules, she has to exist on the smallest possible monthly bursary: 160 dalasis. She resembles the beginning of a novel that is destined to have an unhappy ending. The two African students who are accompanying us for half the journey hanker after the very opposite: away, to Sweden, and sharpish. But there are yet more novels on board. When we are all seated, one small table with two chairs remains unoccupied. The chairs are tipped forward, inclined toward the table, and when their two occupants make their entrance, a child can see why. For this is the bygone world, English of course, big, white and clumsy, with an aura of a life spent in the tropics. He is clad in a pair of those white shorts that come down to his poignant knees. The darned knee-length socks are encased in stout brogues (purchased in Bond Street in 1938), the signet ring on the little finger of his left hand sports the family crest and is in perfect harmony with the darn in his shirt collar. She is sturdy, enveloped in a flowery frock, and with the sort of face that can move mountains. English dog breeders have often striven to reproduce such faces, but they still look better on people.

No harm can come to us now: crocodiles will swerve aside, the ship will not founder, and the tea will always be hot. Mr. Dembo undergoes an instant transformation and cries "Yes, sah! Very good, sah!" as if he wants to show us that there are other whites besides a disorderly group of beer-drinking, tranny-toting Danes.

The meal costs next to nothing, which is just as well because that is what we get. Half the rations probably get resold from the kitchen, but it is a lesson in "how the other half lives." Three minuscule pieces of meat, one pineapple ring shared between four, the remnants of a remnant of a fish, and when the Danes clamor for more they receive another spoonful of rice.

With my cup of Nescafé clasped in my hand, I clamber back on deck. Clamber, because all the lights are out. The ship is moving along in total darkness, no headlight, no searchlight, nothing. After a while I make out the oily surface of the water, and after a bit longer still, I can even see the stars' reflections in it. When someone opens the door of the dining saloon and a shaft of light escapes, an angry yell issues from up in the wheelhouse.

Not only does the river remain tidal until deep within the interior, the invisible channels and banks demand nothing less than the eye of a hawk. It is left up to the ground-nutters and pirogues, also moving about in total darkness, to listen out for our approaching chug-chug-chug in the hush of the night, and make themselves scarce. It is becoming cool on deck. The distant banks must be out there somewhere, but nothing is visible. People lie all over the place, sleeping, on the forward deck, the rear deck, in the gangways; mothers with children, vendors, bearers, sailors, all asleep. Only aft does a tiny carbide lamp glow. In between the sleeping bundles, a bearded face, exuberant hair braided into a charming bun, lies reading *Masters of the XXth Century*. He does not look up, and I cannot get to him because of all the bodies.

The Danes sit with some new-found African friends, smoking huge reefers of *djamba*, whose pungent reek pursues me as far as my cabin. The approach to my door is blocked by prone sleepers.

WHEN I WAKE up I am not sure how much later it is. I hear the soft chug-chug of the engines. But that is not what has woken me. A low crunching sound, as if someone is chewing on too-long nails. I feel behind me for the lamp, and kick off the sweaty sheets. On the rim of the grimy washbasin, a brown cockroach as big as a child's thumb sits staring dreamily at me. "So, Moriarty, we meet at last," I think, and consider what sort of sound it will make when I crush it. So I don't.

Through the screen in front of the porthole I can vaguely make out the light of the moon, and the bodies of the fallen up on deck, and just because, like you, I am the measure of all things, I can at the same time see a map of Africa, massively blown-up to 1:1 scale, and on it the river as a real river with that peaceful, white riverboat softly glugging as it creeps over the invisible water—and on that boat, like the one-thousandth segment of a grapefruit, myself and the cockroach. I bid it goodnight and turn off the light.

WHEN I WAKE again it is six in the morning and still dark. My friend has gone, and the ship is not moving. So I did not dream those two sharp cries. I hear bare feet step outside, pull on some clothes, and go on deck. It is almost chilly. Several figures are standing in the dimness on a ramshackle pier, their dove-gray shapes wrapped in blankets. A few men disembark, stepping into a broad, hollowed-out tree trunk in which a small fire is burning. An old man is selling dried fish from a large basket. A boy goes ashore to buy a couple. They are obviously cheaper here than in Banjul. There is no sign of a village. The unyielding night is draped like a curtain behind the men, they will have to lift it up in order to leave. A high-pitched African voice shouts an order, and a small boy dressed in a jute sack casts off.

Where were we? Albreda, Kerewan, Kemoto, Tendaba, Balligho, Yellitenda, Sankuya, Bai? Breakfast consists of a local version of Gambia's English past: a rasher of bacon, bread dripping in fat, and a plate of porridge that would do a bricklayer credit. The Danes complement it with cognac and beer. Outside, the day has adorned itself with landscapes, Ruysdael-like panoramas glimpsed through Potemkin-walls of mangroves, robbing you of the illusion that you are sailing through forests. Enormous baobabs stand in the empty savannah, leafless at this time of the year, so that it is winter and summer at the same time.

The Big Wheel has appeared on deck in a carmine-red dressing gown, and a white woolly hat with two pompoms. He spreads out a multicolored silk blanket and proceeds to say his morning prayers, so I can tell immediately where east is.

THAT DAY IT gets very hot indeed. We see a hippopotamus, a pelican, monkeys. Wherever we stop whole villages turn out, long lines of people materialize from the empty landscape, greetings and gossip are exchanged, coconuts and cassavas sold, mail handed over, for this is the last floating post office in the world, with its own subpostmaster and its own official stamp: River

Gambia. The hippie on the aft deck, who is called Lechinski and comes from Montreal, says that it is forty degrees centigrade, and ducks beneath the sailcloth sunshade. He explains to Miss Peace Corps how wrong it is, what she is going to do, and why for Africa there can only be African solutions. But he might just as well be explaining to Florence Nightingale that you should never bandage soldiers' wounds. She merely glows the more, determined to make her contribution to Africa's further awakening. I say that Africa never of itself woke up: it was rudely awakened by us. For all we know, it might well have preferred to turn over once more and continue its long, delightful sleep.

Here, far from the miserable imitation-world on the coast—that thin, modernized stratum—you start to feel the breadth and power of the entire continent. We crawl over it like a tiny fly, on the map the distance we are covering is a millimeter, and yet the recollection of town, government, streets, and the relics of colonialism has already irretrievably vanished: one gulp and we are swallowed up by this infinite land. Sometimes we see a settlement, straw huts, or zinc roofs; men sit together beneath plaited roofing, and I long to know what they are discussing. Lunch follows on from coffee, teatime from lunch. Peering through the English couple's binoculars, I see fish eagles and white herons in the shimmering afternoon light. Inside the cabins it is even hotter than in the sun, where, nevertheless, people are sprawled on all the decks, in a sleep that seems further removed from life than any sort of death. The days pass in this fashion until we reach Bassé. We arrive late one night, but remain on board.

In the middle of the night I become aware of something walking over my leg, on little feet of rough tweed. The light won't go on because the engines are not working. I strike a match, see an extremely large spider among the sheets, and go up on deck, full of sorrow that everything has now come to an end. The river continues to Fatoto, Senegal, and other countries, but we are returning to the coast. We sit together for the last time in a sort of innocent melancholy. Lechinski says the "endless" feeling you get in Africa comes from there being no seasons. He steps ashore at daybreak, his long hair flying in the morning breeze. In his hand he holds a small bag, and does not yet know where he is headed. Miss Peace Corps is next to leave. She threatens to break our hearts, for now we are able to see just where she will be spending those two years: a few huts, some buildings, a strip of tarmac road that soon peters out, a fence around a dusty mountain of peanuts, a sandy, wide-open spot on the river. The Danes and Swedes are picked up, the English couple are remaining on board, I am the only one with nowhere to go. Not a Peugeot to be seen! I head into the village. It gets hotter far earlier here than it does in Banjul. A market, St. Joseph's School, the police station, a branch of the Transport

Union. The boss is a towering black man. "Ah, you Mistah Boo! Daddy Soul, he telephone dis morning. Car come to take you, he break down, I can give you pickup."

A PICK-UP, small and open-topped, is pure hell on these roads, but better than nothing. I stipulate that the man must stop when I ask him to, and explain that I paid extra for this. Within an hour I am dehydrated and caked in red dust. The codriver sits beside me in the open back. He has six fingers on each hand and is kindly disposed toward the world. We drink hot ginger ale together and hot soda, which tastes of iron. This is a treat for him—usually as many people as humanly possible are squeezed on to a truck like this. When we reach a village where I want to stop, he leads the way like a guide. The speed at which it all takes place. In no time at all the village chief is standing before me, a book with Arabic lettering folded open, and clasped to his breast. He points to where I should look, and I look. Then we go walkabout, followed by all the inhabitants, who obviously find it a humorous situation, and rightly so, for what am I doing here?

Girls draw water from the depths of a well, there is a tree with vultures and a tree with storks, on the horizon the undergrowth is smoldering and black smoke is drifting this way. The huts are cool and clean; he leads me in and out, steering me gently by my arm. I reflect that life in a village of this sort has been the same for centuries, the rich man with his cattle, the castes (invisible to us) of singers, warriors, smiths. The powwows in the shade of the trees, the work in the fields, the hunting, sitting, and telling stories—no English or French regime has ever succeeded in altering a bit of it, and I leave it as I found it, undisturbed and itself.

The only one to whom anything has happened is me; seeing them has increased the distance, not lessened it. They cannot see my house, although I can see theirs. Walking back to the road, my six-fingered friend picks me plants and twigs, letting me sniff them and giving them names. And I keep looking back at the people who go on standing there, and who have abandoned me to my own fate: someone who will never be an African, who will never know what it is like to sit under a tree at evening time and tell one another long, drawn-out stories, who will never live *in* his family until everything and everybody is used up.

But just what is it that I want? Too much, as usual, which is always bad. And yet, to live just once is a cruel prison. Only on the stage do people seem able to escape this incarceration.

My final stop is at Mansa Konko. A Dutch leprosy doctor is supposed to live there, whom we track down with some difficulty. A few low-lying buildings in a scanty garden. Two blonde, suddenly very white doctors and a Dutch child. It is thirty-eight degrees in the coolest room in the house. We eat cheese sandwiches, Dutch-style. It is a hard way of life, they say, but they enjoy it. I would like to stay longer, talking. Measuring the superficiality of my chance visit against the stamina of people who spend years here, and know more than anyone else what it is like, but the pickup driver does not approve of our tête-à-tête, and begins a claxon concerto.

* * *

ON THE LAST day of my visit I am granted an interview with the vice-president. I spend the remainder of the time hunting for signs from the past. One of them is hanging on the wall of the Anglican Church. "Sacred to the memory of Providence Doyery who departed this life (as if life were an object, or is it?) Nov. 24, 1863, aged 47 y. He was a native of EBOE, a country in Guinea on the West Coast of Africa, was sold, captured and brought (in that

order) to the Gambia in 1829 where he lived and died and was
beloved by all who knew him."

> Weep not! The land to which I go
> Is beautiful and bright
> There shall no tears of sorrow flow
> And there shall be no night.
> Rejoice! We yet shall meet again
> Where none may say "farewell"
> And in the home of deathless love
> Together we shall dwell.

It is a day of doom and death. When I emerge from the faded,
cool church into the blazing light of the street, I come across
Daddy Soul, who is on his way to the funeral of his uncle, the gold-
smith. A pretty mixed bunch are wending their way toward the
cemetery down by the shore, but I am in search of different dead:
a few cement graves in a small, bare plot being meticulously raked
by a prodigiously old man, who will insist on calling me "massa."
The leaves of the acacia flutter down and he rakes them up, just
as a different gardener raked up H. Best and George Pierez when
their plane crashed here in 1944. "Thou shalt know hereafter,"
their grave pronounces ominously, and the acacia leaves continue
to flutter down upon Lt. Col. R.V.M. Garry and Wing Commander
R.O.M. Graham DFC and have done so for even longer upon,
"Margaret, the beloved wife of Richard Pine Esq., formerly the
Queen's Advocate for these settlements, who departed this life on
the last day of the year one thousand eight hundred and forty-two
in the 27th year of her age." Tangled webs and gossamer threads,
all the dust and fragments empires leave behind when they pack
their bags! Boxes of stone containing people, maxims on top,

powdered with the red coral of the *Russelia juncea*, shaded by the pointy, russet leaves of the euphorbia, and at the end of all the dreams, the gardener stands raking.

MEANWHILE THE time for my departure is approaching. I have reached that curious mix of fullness and regret, when there are only two choices left: either you leave immediately or you stay for a year. Anything in between produces a bad piece of writing. A few days after returning from the river I will be suspended above it, and even from up there it looks broad and mighty. An hour or so later I shall be sitting in Dakar drinking Pernod among people with shoes, and already feeling homesick for that which was hot and slow and torpid, and which can never be forgotten.

THE VICE PRESIDENT, Hassan Musa Camara, Minister for Local Govt, Lands and Mines, hoots with merriment when he hears about my difficulties in reaching the president, and phones him up in my presence. He addresses him by the nickname Aichee, and only afterwards do I realize that, phonetically strung together, these are the initials of His Excellency. On the other end of the line, Aichee roars with laughter too, but he is leaving for Moscow the following day, and I am flying to Dakar the same afternoon, so that is that. The friendly, bustling streets of Banjul, with their accompanying heat, seem suddenly far away. We are sitting among the cool pools of power, the air conditioning is humming, and the vice president, by the looks of it an energetic administrator, is giving me an exposé of the ups and downs of a minicountry in the big wide world. "We are a country which was given no chance to survive economically as an independent nation," he says, but he is, nevertheless, highly satisfied with his first balance of payments surplus, even though he is aware that it rests on a single precarious crop, the peanut. This is perilous in the extreme. If world prices drop, they will drag Gambia with them into the quagmire. And there have been many mistakes as well. Not of the golden beds, prestigious palaces, stadiums, and excessive diplomatic representation variety. Quite the contrary. Gambia is adroit and sensible, having only a few diplomats abroad, and maintaining calm at home. The mistake, they now feel, was to have put too much emphasis on the towns and their hinterlands, and to have paid too little attention to the countryside, and thus to domestic food production. The latest plan, an ambitious one, is to teach the Gambians how to fish, on the coast as well as on the river (at present being exploited by the Japanese). But the Gambian, strangely enough, is no fisherman, and is unwilling to abandon his herd. A herd defines your wealth and status and consequently is not there to be slaughtered. All these historically determined attitudes have meant that imports of the primary necessities of life—fish, meat, and agricultural products—have been too high. Much of the income earned by the fledgling Swedish hotel industry flows back to the cold North, due to the monopoly position of the Scandinavian tour operators, itself a monoculture of sorts. In addition, there is the fear that all those liberated, libidinous, well-heeled ladies and gentlemen will corrupt the "African" character of the youth. Camara says he regrets the fact that the opposition has shrunk to a minimum. Opportunism has something to do with this: when capable people see that there is little chance of them getting a look-in for the foreseeable future, they switch parties, just as many (including the president) have changed both their name and their religion. Christians are left in peace, and do of course fill administrative positions within the civil service, but it is better for a politician to be Muslim, and to have an African name.

I ask him about the book *Enter the Gambia, Birth of an Improbable Nation* by the American writer Berkeley Rice. It is banned in the

NOMAD'S HOTEL   51

Gambia because it is somewhat disrespectful toward many digni-
taries, singling out rural elections and parliamentary debates for
particular ridicule. He shrugs his shoulders, and when, back in the
Netherlands, I borrow the book from the library of the Tropical
Institute, I understand why. It is easy to make it all sound laugh-
able, primitive and so forth, but to wish to view it in this way is
arrogant and rather malicious, the attitude of a rich and spoiled
child.

I ask him which international aid organizations are at work in
Gambia and it is a very long shopping list, starting with the UN
Development Fund (whose staff live in the splendid, almost colonial isolation of the lush coastal gardens near the British High
Commission), and continuing all the way down to the AID. "They
all do their bit," he says. Later on I look at some of the UNDF literature: it ranges from "hotel-staff training, labour statistics and
man-power planning, study [of] basic environment, sewerage and
drainage" up to and including "the exploitation of kaolin deposits."
Experts arrive, scholarships are given, and everyone beavers away
manfully in the margin of the world, without an army, without a
dictatorship, and without too many temper tantrums. These are
saved up for me on my last day. I have to return the rented bicycle,
which has conveyed me around for part of my time here, and am
approaching that dusty peanut depot on the main road, which
runs along by the sea, when I see some commotion up ahead. A
policeman is waving his arms about. Slowly, in order to avoid a
couple of deep potholes, I cycle off the road. Alas! Too slowly! A
big black Mercedes, which could not contain anyone but Aichee,
sweeps by through the peanut dust, and a minute later I am under
arrest. The officer in his shorts is very angry. True, I did dismount
when "the President of this Country" passed by, *but not quickly
enough*. Wheeling my bicycle beside me, I trudge after him through
the loose sand, forty degrees centigrade. An endearingly Dutch

dispute, which provides a small group of onlookers with a great deal of pleasure. Only after a long wait, much shouting, and an unpleasant confrontation with the mugshots of "other murderers," am I released, having been severely cautioned and had my statement taken. A certain redressing of the cosmic balance seems to have occurred: this time not only have I written about them, but they have written about me too. Two days later, at a sweltering Dakar airport, I see a very different type of officer: grossly overweight Russian pilots, adorned with medals. This time they are not coming for me—it is Aichee who disappears inside the pocket-sized turboprop sent from Moscow by Mr. Brezhnev. But scour as I might, Aichee's Moscow trip does not make the world's press; it is probably too much trouble even to try and explain where the Gambia is. Or, as someone at the Ministry of Foreign Affairs in The Hague said to me, "Gambia? *Gambia?* Oh, you mean Zambia."

SEPTEMBER 1975

Musings in Munich

SOME CITIES LIVE up to their responsibilities. They supply the traveler with the image he has of them, even if it is a false one. This traveler, having left behind the statue of the Angel of Peace on top of the Maximilianeum (he can still feel the golden wave of her goodbye on his back), is strolling past the seductive green of the English Garden toward the Prinzregentenstrasse. He is susceptible to the martial element of the town in which he finds himself. Feldherrenhalle, Siegestor, Ruhmeshalle, the tomb of Ludwig of Bavaria whose black marble was christened a *castrum doloris*, a fortress of suffering, by its sculptor—things military are never far away in Munich. It comes through in the clothing worn by passers-by as well: striking hats, captured feathers, green coats. It is as though the wearers of such garments, perhaps precisely because they are a minority, move through the town with strategic deliberation, each on their mission. Those are not uniforms, they are traditional dress, a German friend explained to him—but still, there is something armor-plated about the people who are so clad. Those *loden* coats of thick, heavily fulled wool, for instance, iron people in reinforced coats.

It has a primordial feel to it. *Halali*, muffled shots in a *finster Wald*, a dark forest, campfires, unintelligible songs. The traveler has seen a photograph of Heidegger in traditional dress. Not that he wishes to draw any modish conclusions from this, after all he too has posed in *Volendammer* costume, and when he did he looked merely comical. Unlike Heidegger. Could you don a sort of uniform, for that was surely what it was, to match your thoughts? And was this the same man who had written about boredom, being, and time, and who had dared to wind strings of words about the void!

You will see what you want to see, his friend had said, and that was just it. You could hardly dispense with yourself, and even before deciding to look there were memories to contend with of what you had once seen, different uniforms against the same, still wholly recognizable backdrop, marches, and parades. He quickened his pace all the same when he heard faint fragments of martial music coming from the direction of the Hofgarten. It was something he felt slightly ashamed of: military music had always excited him. He crossed a big arterial road by way of a Bailey bridge and arrived at a ruin. The music had stopped; a group of young soldiers was standing there, keeping as still as possible. Words floated to him on the breeze, death and remembrance. It was all to do with the war that simply refused to die, which would only disappear when the last person with the taste of it still in their mouth was dead. Only then. There were old men down there, persons who could never have been young, not the ones from the *Sondermeldungen* and *Kriegsjournale*, not the soldiers he had seen as a child, marching behind a similar sort of banner, but different, the same sort of standard, but different. The eagle on this standard was silver, but the mysterious symbol had fallen from its talons; that no longer existed now. He felt his age mingling with that of the elderly men below who had formed themselves into a sort of square. Strange as it seemed, he had more in common with those men than with the young soldiers. He could not hear the words, but it was not necessary anyway, he knew them well enough. Honor, loyalty, mourning, sacrifice, once, then. These men cherished a *then* so as to have a *now*, and their *then* looked like flowers, banners, blue and white ribbons. All this in an enclosure, near a quarry, in front of a ruin—a body of men tugging at time. He goes slowly down the steps toward the Hofgarten.

It was almost as if he had planned it. As he reaches the bottom and enters the Hofgarten itself the young soldiers are rounding a corner, in the way that only marching soldiers can: within the curve a normal person would make they turn at an angle of ninety degrees. And no, they are not the same uniforms, and yes, the chap who bears the standard with the eagle—sunlight reflecting on his silver—*is* tall and blond, and no, the orders are not barked, they are almost spoken, and no, the music does not sound warlike, rather *en sourdine* (as Louis Couperus, the late nineteenth-century Dutch novelist, would say), muffled, muted, and no, there is no stamping, for when the music stops he sees how the big boots, clodhoppers, are lowered in step and almost cautiously onto the loose gravel, making a nearly rhythmic rustling sound. He thinks back to his own past, almost fifty years ago now, a triumphal entry, more men, the uniforms a deeper, more fundamental gray. That lot, they had worn helmets which practically covered their eyes, so that the face had disappeared and they had lost their personalities, exchanged them for an unbearable sameness in which each had become the other.

And, the traveler mused, aware of how time was simultaneously turning his own hair gray, pushing him down, making his bones older, and clouding his eyes until he would be like someone scanning the horizon for that far-off place he himself must have come from, the standards used to be taller, there had been brass, the mouths had sung something to a melody he would never,

ever forget. These heads wore no helmets, they seemed almost adolescent, *pueri imberbi*, to him. They had difficulty keeping in step and their uniforms belonged to some forgotten mini-principality, the gray too light, as though they were choirboys and should have been singing, except that nobody sang, just the rustling of all those feet and the filing past of those shy faces, and the elderly man in front of him who removed his hat, bowed to the standard and straightened up again, so that the traveler felt a twinge of pain in his own back, which was no longer up to such maneuvers; and then it was all over.

He took a step back into the excessively trimmed shrubbery, misshapen flowers and plants that were supposed to portray the national colors, let the old men go by, lost in their indefinable, untranslatable thoughts, and turned round. The angelus began to sound and he caught himself thinking of a Latin phrase. It seemed as though in his life it never got any later.

He walked past park benches where people sat in the autumn sunshine as if intent on stocking up for the Alpine winter. They looked peaceful, sunk in daydreams or meditations, their eyes shut. In a while they would become anonymous passers-by once more, but now, because of their defenselessness, faces given over to the light, they were their own vulnerable selves, city dwellers in a garden—that regimented imitation of nature. Just as he turned aside in order to make his way to the colonnade, where he wanted to see the poems written on the walls, someone appeared who gave the early afternoon a very different feel. He was reminded of the past once more, evidently this was where the majority of his reference points lay. But this man was himself the product of another age. He wore a straw hat and light-colored clothes and had one of those dogs with him which is three-quarters fluff. They said "Good afternoon" as if they were acquainted, or at any rate would have no trouble understanding one another. "What nonsense!" the old man said, and the traveler knew instantly that he was referring to the military ceremony.

Where do I know him from? wondered the traveler, and realized at the same moment that he did not know him as an individual, only as an idea, a species, or whatever you call it. No, not a species, an extinct species. Actor. Variety theater, operetta, why, even Schnitzler himself. Someone who had survived it all. He recalled photographs he must have seen during the war. The photographs had been colored in; then, too, the rose in the lapel of the white Palm Beach suit would have been red. Names ran through his head as well: Hans Moser, Heinz Rühmann, Moser's nasal tone, that strange Viennese accent. He had not replied, nor was it necessary. Memories. Paul Steenbergen in a play by Anouilh, the heyday of Dutch theater, a world which nowadays seemed to have fallen into the hands of puerile talents. The old man chuckled, as though he knew what the other was thinking. His face was cultured, cheerful, ironic. They uttered a few sentences that someone had written for them, and which meant nothing save that they appreciated being able to carry on this semblance of a conversation. Then the other one took off his hat, waved it about a bit in the blue air, said *"Sehr verehrt"* or something like that, and turned on his heel precisely in the middle of the broad path, just as a director would have instructed. There was no one else there now. The dog followed him and he watched them go, how they kept to that straight line over the shadows of the trees and the light patches in between, holding a course between the grass borders on either side of the path. This man knew what he would look like from behind should someone be watching him leave—he knew how to *position* himself. He was also aware that the effect of his walking away would be ruined if he turned round, or chose one of the side paths.

What was it that he found so moving about it? A presence

from a vanished world? He thought of other old men whom he had known, one of whom had died recently—the father of a friend, Jewish, cosmopolitan, as old as the century, originating from this same country, perhaps even the same place, driven out in the 1930s by the others, the memory of whom is palpable here. Perhaps it was the sheer mass of memory that affected him, all those notions contained in names, parks, statues, triumphal arches that had interfered with his past too; indeed, it seemed as though you could not take a single step in this part of the world—his part of the world—without being confronted with fragments, intimations, exhortations to mourn or reflect. The past as profession, a form of sickness surely? Normal people were concerned with the future, or with the floating iceberg they called life, that moving-picture show which belonged nowhere, was always on the move. On that iceberg he was the one who looked back. Everything in Europe was old, but here in the middle of the land mass the age seemed to have a different specific gravity. He was making his way through a vanished kingdom, not that this gave rise to any special sentiments in itself, no, once he reached the East, that was when it would begin in earnest; the crushed, shattered world of Musil, of King and Kaiser, all those bits, fragments, the impotence of power, the hermetically sealed world of Poland and Czechoslovakia that seemed to have been torn from the Continent, then there was Serbia, Croatia, Slovenia, and Trieste, and the sheer force of what had happened to those regions in the twentieth century, was still happening, the twice-lost worlds of Isaac Bashevis Singer and Vladimir Nabokov, of Kafka and Rilke, Roth and Canetti. It seemed to him that here was the lookout post from where you could gaze far back into time and see just how much these regions had once belonged, could see just how deep the wound was. Trying to reach it meant climbing down a mine shaft. He never had that feeling in France or Italy, or in his own country. Past enough there too, yet it seemed somehow to have been converted by more or less organic process into the present. Here that other part had not made it, had got stuck, bogged down, torn away. But it still existed, perhaps it was waiting. The wind he could feel on his face came from there, hot, searing, as if it too wanted to say something. The old man had disappeared from sight by now. "What nonsense," he had said, but now—now that he and his light-hearted guise had vanished— those words lingered on the air, so much less innocent than when he had uttered them. What had taken place here, in this town, that beginning, more than sixty years ago, could never come under the heading of "nonsense," unless, that is, you took the word literally for once, as in "non-sense," the negation of sense, which had nothing to do with madness, even though there was a preference for using it to label that period, on the grounds of *non compos mentis* which it implied. An absence of sense; then, once. That had been the end, an end that still went on and that, if his friends were to be believed, was about to be reversed. But, the traveler thought, the servants of the past do not travel well in the future, and set course for the towers of the Teatinerkirche, whose color put him in mind of the pudding they used to serve at boarding school and according to the pupils was made on January 1st for the whole year.

Boarding school, Augustinians, pudding, food. It is busy under the frosted-glass cupola of Restaurant Augustiner in the Neuhausstrasse. The waitresses are in traditional dress, low-cut, white, puffy blouses. They stuff the bills into their bodices, between their Bavarian breasts. The choir of the Czardasfürstin, embroidered aprons, red sash, leg-of-mutton sleeves. Female traditional dress seems not to bother him at all. Carp in dark beer batter and potatoes fried with herbs and butter. Lollo Rosso lettuce with diced potatoes. Franconian black pudding and liver sausage. Franconian potato soup with mushrooms and marjoram, one quarter Franconian roast goose with handmade potato dump-lings, red cabbage or celery salad, three pieces of potato waffles with apple purée, stuffed baked apple.

Country fare in the middle of town, something that no longer exists in his country, but then in his country there was hardly any countryside left anyway. The list of dishes sounded like an incantation of typical national qualities, and why was that simul-taneously repellent and attractive? "Nationalistic," a word that is linked with hatred, but also with tradition, preservation in the sense of saving up, not throwing away, letting things remain for a time within time, a postponement of the demise of the discern-ible world. Why were some forms of preservation acceptable (brown bears in Spain, sparrowhawks and badgers in Holland) while others—national dress, languages, dances, dishes—were regarded with suspicion? Both forms had to do with a wilful-ness that toiled against the direction of time's arrow, impotent final attempts. The suspicious side was probably the misuse that occurred when human affairs were involved, or when the word *Blut* was added, mixed in with its twin brother *Boden*. It was evidently impossible to consider such things without, as he called it, going through the repertoire. The mind, that thinking and feeling authority, was unable to get on with the job without first engaging with its more or less automatic upper layer, where this repertoire lay. The repertoire housed the *idées reçues*—the received ideas—what everybody had to say about everything, a whole series of platitudes to be got through before the real thinking began.

He knew he would not reach this stage that afternoon; there was too much to see, and seeing, because of the superficial catego-rizing that went with it, belonged to the repertoire.

A punk was sitting nearby, female, with a towering black cock's comb above her innocent face; a podgy girl disguised as a gladiator. He noticed that she repeatedly asked for apple purée, baby food. The waitress was kind to her, mothering. Categories, halfway houses to what he regarded as thought. To see, that was why he was here. An older man in traditional dress, with a thick book and a stoup full of beer. If he watched long enough he would see them all, as in the dramatis personae: "Several Soldiers, the Priest, the Lady, an Upper-class Family." He glanced toward the old man engrossed in his book, and was inevitably reminded again of Heidegger. Traditional dress was perhaps a mild enough form of anachronism. Some people continued wearing things that other people in the same period no longer wore, although everyone had once worn it. Heidegger had refused to recognize time as a series of consecutive *now*-moments, seeing it as a connection between what had once taken place, *then, before,* and what will take place at *some time, one time,* in the future. The traveler, who had never felt particularly comfortable in the here and now, it being in his nature to regard it as tinged and defined by the past, recognized much in this way of thinking. And those bits of past that did not belong to one's own life nevertheless made huge demands on that life, this was unavoidable, although most people seemed to manage perfectly well without thinking about the past, and entire countries apparently found it easy enough when circumstances dictated, to forget it. He never did have much to say about the future except, no matter how dark the past often seemed, it was impossible for him to be a pessimist. As far as he was concerned humanity was a collection of mutants on their way to an invisible goal that might not even exist. The problem was that they were not going there in synchronized fashion. While some still found themselves in the Middle Ages of fundamentalism, others were sitting behind their computers or on their way to Mars. Not that this mattered, it was the hybrid forms halfway between the two that were so explosive: the instruments of one lot in the hands of the other, the terrorist who wishes to take his enemy with him in his act of suicide because he believes that by doing this he will gain entry to paradise.

But was it really true that he had never felt at home in the present? That would be romanticism and a trifle childish. It was more a question of not feeling at home between people who felt at home exclusively in the present, who pinned all their hopes on it. If you were not able, perhaps paradoxically, to free yourself of it, then it had no taste. The past had been steeped in lye, the extraneous removed—not something that could be said of the present. For the last time (and only because the gentleman in traditional dress was seated opposite, reading) he thought of the photograph of Heidegger in his peculiar costume. Nietzsche had said that philosophy frequently had physical causes, and the traveler wondered if the philosopher's body had felt comfortable in that traditional dress, which, like his theories, pointed so insistently to the past. But perhaps that was going too far, although now, as he ordered an *Oberberger Vulkanfelsen*, he was back with the *Blut* and *Boden* again, for the wine was a blood red and once you added that name you felt you were quaffing a volcanic rock.

Seeing blood in wine, that had to be his Catholic upbringing. Besides, why had he chosen *that* particular wine? Language takes note of the psyche: after all he might just as well have ordered a Randersackerer Ewigleber '86 or a Rödelseer Schwanleite. The deconstruction of wine names, someone should get on to that. He looked at the ferns, the bronze busts, the baskets of dried Alpine flowers hanging from the ceiling. Stags' antlers, potted lime trees, ornaments made of shells. He was in different territory. All around him he could hear the Bavarian version of German, and for the first time he realized German must have been the first foreign language he ever heard.

Sixteen years before, in a white clapboard country house in Maine, an old man—white-haired once again and reminiscent of his friend's dead father and thus of the old man who had spoken to him in the park—had asked him to read some Rilke out loud. This man had had the same accent in English as his friend's father in Dutch. A German accent, but more than German, an entire Middle European past was contained within it, an indestructible, thick, attractive accent, even his friend who had lived in the Netherlands for so long still bore traces of it. That request in Maine had taken him aback, partly because his host, who had been awarded the Nobel Prize for a discovery in biochemistry, was someone he looked up to enormously. When he heard the traveler was from the Netherlands he had immediately started talking about Multatuli, the nineteenth-century Dutch author, thus shutting out all the American guests. He came across this more often, people over eighty who would hold forth on Multatuli or Couperus; the Netherlands really had existed once. But with regard to Rilke his host had been implacable. The traveler had protested that his German was not up to it, but the old man had refused to give this any countenance. Thanksgiving, November, Indian Summer, the entire garden, which stretched as far as Penobscot Bay, aflame with color. He had opened the book, yellowed, falling to bits, signs of nostalgia on every page, at the place where he was required to read from—and he had read. The Americans had kept very quiet, he could hear the fire crackling in the grate, but he had not read for the others, just for that white head bent over and thinking of God knows what, something from fifty years before, when he had not yet been driven out or forced to flee, something *old*, and when he read, it was as if a globe with ancient air had been revealed and his own voice was mingling with that rarefied, carefully preserved, ancient air:

> *Lord, it is time. The summer was too long.*
> *Lay your shadow on the sundials now,*
> *and through the meadow let the winds throng.*
>
> *Ask the last fruits to ripen on the vine;*
> *give them further two more summer days*
> *to bring about perfection and to raise*
> *the final sweetness in the heavy wine.*
>
> *Whoever has no house now will establish none,*
> *whoever lives alone now will live on long alone,*
> *will waken, read, and write long letters,*
> *wander up and down the barren paths*
> *the parks expose when the leaves are blown.*

He had read more that late afternoon, but during the final lines of this poem he had seen how the lips of his host were moving in time to his own, and he had been touched, a feeling which now came over him again, as though no gap could possibly exist between that *then* and this *now*. The old man was dead, as was his friend's father, plus a few more of those men who seemed constantly to cross his path, as though a rare form of predestination was involved. All of them had lived beyond eighty. A cellist, a restorer of paintings, a banker. Survival had wrapped itself about them like a second soul, not the surviving itself, for all five of them were now dead, but rather that which they had survived, and about which not one of them had ever spoken to him.

BUT THIS WAS Munich. He had not come here to recall all this, but to look. Yet as he sat there quietly with his glass of Volcano wine he seemed to be caught up in the eye of a storm of memories. How strange it was. Time itself, that weightless thing, could only go in one direction, no matter how you defined it or tried to step on its tail—that much at least seemed certain. Nobody knew what time was, but even if you placed all the clocks in the world in a circle, time would still run straight on, and should there be a finite end to time it was not one that could be imagined by human beings without a severe case of vertigo. But what then were memories? Time that had been left behind and had now caught up with you, or that you yourself, by moving against the tide of time—doing the impossible, in fact—could retrieve. And not just your own memories, those of others as well. His friend's father, for instance, who had been a friend of Toller,* once told him how he had been present during Toller's failed revolution in Munich. It had taken place here, where the traveler was now, with all the violence, screaming, and death that would have been part of it. After that, Toller went into exile, first to London, then New York. His friend had once pointed out the Mayflower Hotel to him: "That's where Toller committed suicide." But the ultimate irony was that long after Toller's death, his friend's father had gone to see a play in Amsterdam about Toller. The survivor had gone to watch an actor playing his dead friend, but that evening the Stadsschouwburg Theater was targeted by Dutch drama students taking part in a protest action, the so-called *Actie Tomaat*; shouting, tear gas, abandoned performance, and with tears in his eyes the old man had left the theatre, the true revolution driven out by the pseudo variety. He could see his friend's father quite clearly now. Even in

---

* Ernst Toller (1893–1939), German dramatist, socialist, revolutionary.

his late eighties he had remained a handsome man, a real presence, slightly bowed, dark eyes, the face of an old Indian, a mane of white hair. In Thomas Mann's diaries he is regularly referred to. "Dr L—— came to visit. We had some delicious spinach." "Yes," his son had said, "but what did you talk about? There's no mention of that." When memory refuses to work it is as if the time in which that lost memory took place has never existed, and perhaps it has not. Time itself is nothing, the experiencing of it everything. When that dies away, it takes the form of a negation, the symbol of mortality—that which you lose before you lose it all. When his friend said as much to his father the response had been: "If you had to remember everything you would burst. There just isn't room enough. Forgetting is a medicine, you have to take it in time."

In time. As he stood up and made his way outside through the spacious dining room of the restaurant he had to smile at himself. For heaven's sake, how could you possibly reflect on a concept that had wormed its way into the language in a thousand different ways, thus enabling it to obscure any image you might form of it? Time has always been muddled up with the instruments used to measure it. Always. In one of the Scandinavian languages the word translates as "the whole time," as if one could ever say that about something which was not yet complete. Human time, scientific time, Newton's version—which proceeded uniformly and without any relation to external objects—Einstein's, which allowed itself to be bewitched by space. And then, too, there was the endless tiny-particles variety—the pulverized, incalculable reduction. He glanced at the others, milling solidly around him on Neuhausstrasse, each with their inner clock, upon which the clock on their wrist attempted vainly to impose its miserable order. Watches were boasters; they claimed to speak *with* authority *for* an authority no one had (yet) ever seen. Still, they did know what time the church doors opened, and a moment later (later—there was no getting away from the tyrant) he was standing in the cool interior of the Sankt Michaelskirche. The first word he read was "Uhr" of course: "On 22 November 1944 shortly after 1 PM St. Michael's Church was hit by several American air force bombs," and here too the memories came flooding back—the heavy sound of the bombers flying over Holland during the war and the eager excitement of the grown-ups: "There go the Americans, they're off to bomb the Hun." That sound, it belonged to those things which were etched on the mind for good because it had to do with death and revenge—the entire vault of heaven one endless basso continuo, played by a musician bent on destruction. But he did not want to think about that now. The dead were dead, the church had been rebuilt, and through the filtered, light gray space a woman was walking purposefully toward her objective. She was dressed splendidly. All in black, her light blonde hair in a chignon bound with a black velvet ribbon. She knelt, her face buried in her hands. Her patent leather shoes did not quite reach the ground and hung there just above it. The sun went in at that moment, the plaster vaulting dulled over, and he saw how three Japanese tourists stared at the woman. At the back of the church a bronze angel leaned against a large christening font, nonchalantly, like someone passing a piano and pausing for a minute to play a few bars. He could see praying figures everywhere; they emphasized the magnitude of the building, beseeching dwarfs in red and hunting green. A farmer in traditional dress stood with his hand on his heart and said something to an effigy, but the traveler made his way back to the angel and went and stood next to him, two casual churchgoers, a man and an angel, one with wings and one without. The angel was bigger and his bronze shone, but that did not matter. He studied the spread-out fingers, and then the wings. This was his second angel today, but this one was no woman. Angels were men in the dictionary; they had men's names, Lucifer, Gabriel, Michael, but they were not men. They were myriads, or so he had been taught, and they came in many forms. Of darkness, of doom, of light. Keepers, messengers. They had ranks, Cherubim and Seraphim, powers, thrones. Heavenly legions. He could not remember whether he had ever really believed in them, he thought not. But it was an attractive idea. Somebody who did not have to be human, but still resembled them, did not have to grow old and, what is more, could fly. Of course, there was all sorts of stuff they were not allowed to do; that was on the cards when you flew so close to God. What he liked was the fact that they were still around, and not just in churches. Made of wood, stone, bronze, on Monuments to the Dead and for Peace, worldly buildings too—they had managed to hold their own all over the place. The Muslims had them as well. Did people still see them? Or had they become, despite their superhuman size and apparentness, invisible? He did not think so; he suspected the others did not see them as he did, by design, but perceived them as you do in a dream, so that the wingéd ones were able to find their way to the secret spaces where the nameless forefathers lived, without the recipient actually noticing. But here he was again, back with an idea related to time, something he had now really had enough of. He had promised himself one more church that day; this one, he felt, belonged more to the town than that falsely nostalgic reconstruction of a wounded Athens, and he was on his way to see it. The church was supposed to be on Sendlingerstrasse, but suddenly up popped the tour guide, who wanted to steer him in the opposite direction.

"Where to then?" He said it irritably, for he had entirely forgotten the man's existence. He must have been hiding under the table when he was in the restaurant. Could someone like this hear all your thoughts too?

"To the Viktualienmarkt," the guide said.

Markets, like cemeteries, were his weakness, and he followed without complaint. Food was perhaps the thing that was furthest removed from evil. All those radishes, cabbages, cheeses, loaves of bread, mushrooms, pumpkins, and eggs evoked the idea of nature, a pastoral type of patience, bang in the center of town. They reminded a town of its origins as a marketplace in a country area, and he wandered around for half an hour among the piled-up produce, the fresh herbs, the sausages—their endless varieties defying the imagination—sides of bacon, fish from the lakes and rivers, all of which looked just the same as it had done a thousand years before. The thousand-year-old kingdom of carrots, carp, and onions, who continued to offer themselves unstintingly to be ground between human teeth.

The street where the church was situated was a busy one, but once inside he left the noise behind. St. Johannes Nepomuk, the guide had whispered. A Bohemian saint. The traveler liked that word, *Bohemian*. Not only because it sounded so attractive but also because of the misunderstandings it brought with it. Because the first gypsies in France were taken for followers of Jan Hus, the heretic from Bohemia, various painters and poets were still labeled *bohemian* to this day. An amalgamation of prejudices based on a misunderstanding, it did not come better than that, and the fact that poets had been identified with vagrants, gypsies, and heathens was pretty good too.

"Nepomuk," the guide repeated. Once the most popular saint in Bavaria apart from Mary. Tortured to death, drowned in the

Moldau, six hundred years ago. Because the traveler felt he was to some degree from Bohemia himself, he decided to adopt the unknown Nepomuk as his patron saint. The guide was now attempting to shower him with information about the saint's life, including what was carved in the wood of the portal doors, but the traveler had already been spirited away by the wondrous space in which he found himself. He would listen and learn later, not now, now he wanted to be waltzed around something he would once have scorned as frills and froth. The baroque, like opera, had been a late discovery in his life; he used to find it impossible to understand what people saw in it, and he still found it difficult to put into words. There was no need to be ashamed about it—to err was human, after all. But here? Perhaps it was the superabundance, and at the same time, in contrast, the strict framework within which it was permitted. Voluptuous. Full. And, perhaps the most difficult thing for a lover of Romanesque churches to admit, *cozy, homely*. Even if you were there alone it felt as though all sorts of things were going on; angels jostling, garments flapping, wind whipping up the stone, marble and gilded plaster, hustle and bustle, a stalactite cave in which belief and the Works of God had got caught on every protuberance. Festoons, fluted columns, riotous crypts, curving lines, perhaps here he was seeing the soul of Bavaria for the first time. The Athens of the Königsplatz had been imposed, thought up by others, while here, at a pinch, you could even yodel because the building itself was doing something like that—trilling, exulting, crazy high Cs. The Bohemian saint was celebrated in the retables around the altar, a swaying, swerving life in which the tellers had little desire to come straight to the point. Carve, French polish, embellish, invert, interrupt—it wriggles while standing still. As hectic as a heavenly crossroads. God with tiara bends over the cross, flanked by two angels whose wings point upright, pricked-up donkey's ears. As there is no one around he steps away from the altar, craning his neck. It strikes him that if you try to look as perpendicularly upwards as possible, beyond the pilasters, golden capitals, flowery festoons, and tubby columns of the balustrade, and then move your head gradually to one side, more and more of those idiotic-cherubic faces come into view. They live here, obviously. When he moves they do too, looking down at him with an improper, far too grown-up expression of ecstasy on their plaster features. It is, he thinks, as if the wall up there has begun to foam and froth, and the froth has assumed a human guise. Quite unbidden, a line of Goethe's on movement, remembered from a Schubert song, occurs to him: *"Was bedeutet die Bewegung?"* (What does that movement signify?) And that is perhaps also the answer: here, meaning lies entirely within movement itself, this is the furthest one can go in expressing movement in static material, movement and stasis, the coagulation of utmost exuberance.

DOES HE KNOW the town better now? He's not sure, but he decides that this is the moment to leave. Where to? South, in the wake of the migratory birds who woke him this morning. To another Bohemia somewhere, to the mountains—the watershed of Europe—where the languages, the states, the rivers flow in all directions, the part of his continent he loves the most, with its chaos of lost kingdoms, reconquered territories, colliding languages, clashing systems, the contradiction of valleys and mountains, the ancient, splintered realm of the Middle. He makes his way again across the lush grass of the English Garden, sees the trees in the last fire of autumn, feeds the swans, lies down on the green and watches the clouds moving toward the Alps. No, he does not yet know this town, but right now other towns are calling him, and that cry which is audible to nobody else—the secret sing-song of Bohemians—is one he cannot resist.

MARCH 1989

The Stones of Aran

THE VOICE ACCOMPANYING the film spoke about the earliest Christian monks who had journeyed to Ireland, holy communities who had lived here on these barren islands, spoke too about St. Colm and St. Enda, "the church of the four beauties" and the ruins of the "seven churches."

All these images and stories, having precious little to do with a modern reality, had caused me to position these strange islands far away in the ocean. In my imagination, though they were still a part of Ireland, they had become virtually inaccessible outposts, rather like the Hebrides, but even more far-flung, monastic islands somewhere in the middle of the Atlantic nothingness.

I had never been to Ireland, but I had read Yeats, Synge, and Joyce, and had translated into Dutch the plays of Brendan Behan and Sean O'Casey from which I had retained some vague, poetical notions. I thought of Ireland as a country where literature and poetry were held in higher esteem than anywhere else in Europe. But only recently were these notions confirmed when I discovered that all the seats on my Aer Lingus plane were upholstered in facsimiles of the handwriting of Joyce and Beckett, Wilde and Swift on a green background, and that nothing in Ireland was ever quite like anywhere else. This did not just apply to the upholstery of the aircraft seats or the countless writers' portraits in dark, cozy pubs, but to the geography as well.

For the mythical distance I had created in my mind between the mainland and the three Aran Islands was but a small distance on the map, although this small distance could, according to Irish friends, suddenly become unpleasantly large if you were stuck on one of the islands with the boat unable to make the crossing due to bad weather, something that apparently occurred regularly.

Of my first trip, which could only be a brief one, I remember rain, and darkness falling early. I had found a room with difficulty on Inishmore (there are no hotels), the largest of the three islands. It was raining and the afternoon was already darkening; two pony-and-traps and a few vans stood on the quay, but my under- standing was that my lodgings were in Kilronan itself, where the boat docked. During the crossing someone had drawn me a map of such simplicity that of course I was unable to find a thing; gusts of wind attempted to lift me off the road, I walked the wrong way—along a muddy, pebbly path that petered out into nothing, and then found it after all, a bed and breakfast run by a young woman whose husband had, in her own words, disappeared to the mainland "for good," leaving her with two children who were still at school, which meant that she stayed open in winter as well.

A short while later I was in my twee little room, which was done up in those lollipop colors so beloved of landladies, who seem to think their guests adore them; a rose nylon bedspread with white appliqué flowers, beige wallpaper with green leaves, a depiction of an abnormally rosy child next to a geranium; it all seemed like a desperate attempt to keep the wintry fury of the squalling storm at bay.

My landlady said that I would be soaked through within minutes and she was right. Disguised as a rain cloud, I blustered into the first pub I came to, my umbrella inside out. Everybody turned to gaze at the stranger. They each had one of those enor- mous glasses of almost black beer, which always makes me think more of food than of drink, in front of them. The television was showing something melodramatic that seemed to come from another world, if only because it was in English while the occasional words wafting from the bar sounded so much more mysterious. Until now I had not heard Gaelic spoken anywhere in Ireland, although everyone told me they had had to learn it at school, but now I heard it for myself. Language is always a puzzle because there is usually no convincing explanation of why things have the names they have, let alone why the very same things a thousand kilometers further away are called something quite different, but there is always something rather poignant about people looking at you and addressing you while you do not understand a word. Suddenly the entire system has been sabotaged, what was designed for communication has become the opposite.

A man came over and sat at my table, he said something to me and in so doing turned me into a very small child, a dog, or a foreigner—for these three are none of them capable of understanding what you say, and each of them evokes a sort of pity on account of their ignorance. It did not matter, he said, if necessary he could speak English to me. Did I understand English? Yes, I understood English, and a short while later I knew his name was Angus and that he had been a fisherman for well on seventeen years, that he had never learned to read ("Aye, that was how it used to be"), that the sea around the island was the most dangerous in the world, so he considered himself very lucky as he had never learned to swim either, which made seventeen years of fishing for mackerel, rockfish, and pollock a bit of a gamble, although mind you, if your *curragh* turned over in this swell you would not stand a chance, even if you could swim. A *curragh*? Those are boats we used to make ourselves, with hulls of light wood and canvas treated with tar, you still see them. And what are you doing tomorrow? It's going to rain again, but not the whole day. You should visit Dun Angus tomorrow. Dun

Angus, Dún Aonghasa, Dún Aengus, I subsequently saw it spelled several different ways. He pointed to a smoke-blackened photograph to one side of the bar, of a vast dark mass of stone which I recognized from that film I had once seen. Yes, tomorrow it would be stormy again, but he could get to within a few yards of it in his van. And it was a must, everyone went there.

I took a look at the photograph and it occurred to me that I would be visiting the island of my imagination after all. Tomorrow, then. Yes, tomorrow.

In the silence which descended for a moment while the television attempted to digest something, I heard the thin, reedy sound of a church bell. Seven o'clock, Holy Mass, my new friend said and held seven fingers aloft and said it again, but this time in Gaelic, *seacht*, and I left the pub and fell in behind a few people walking in the direction of the bell, with the feeling I was doing something special.

Once upon a time Latin-speaking monks had landed here, and the essence of what they brought had been preserved. A different language, the same words. A different time, the same forbidding block of stone. The church was not large yet its interior was surprisingly spacious. The Mass was in Gaelic. I knew what was being said, but I couldn't understand a word. The dark days before Christmas, the priest's chasuble, the mauve of advent the only color among all that stone. The sermon echoed about me, a language of shells and stones, ancient words that penetrated all the surrounding heads and shut me out, but it did not matter, I could sense the community of the others, a product of centuries of isolation and extreme poverty. The unending struggle for food, fish from a jealous, dangerous ocean, earth scraped from between rocks and spread upon layers of seaweed and sand so as to grow a few potatoes, livestock on the few patches of fertile ground, always enclosed by walls of piled stones which first had to be hewn out and dragged there, light from oil lamps until well into the last century, oil obtained from the livers of sharks and seals, houses made of the stone upon which they stood, roofs of rye straw. Even though times have now changed, all this is still visible on faces that continue to bear the stamp of life as a hazardous undertaking.

The following day Angus drives me to the big fort. The road is narrow and he takes me to the spot from where I am to proceed on foot. It seems very odd to me. I spend my summers on a Spanish island where the ground is just as rocky. There, too, each parcel of land is divided from its neighbor by drystone walls. Only there the light during summer hurts your eyes, the ground is dry, and sometimes there is not a drop of rain for weeks, so that it seems this place where I am now is the northern counterpart of my summers. The grass is idiotically green, but as I climb on toward the fort I squelch through brownish mud full of the cloven-hoofed imprints of cattle. No one is sure how ancient the fort is—neither word, nor inscription has survived. It stands high above the ocean, impregnable, protected from the rear by successive walls, and fields full of *chevaux de frise*, large, extremely sharp stones positioned in the ground at a slant, impassable to any horseman. They remind me of the pieces of metal stuck into the ground at the same acute angle on the Potsdamer Platz near the Berlin Wall that were supposed to prevent people fleeing to the West. There are no floors, no halls. Whether or not "fort" is the correct word I am not sure. Standing in the grass among the piled masses of stone, 270 feet above the ocean raging beneath, I find it difficult to imagine the people who built this edifice and the life that was once lived here.

When I arrive back at the van Angus asks me whether I have

seen *Man of Aran*, the film that was shot on the island. He talks about it as though it were yesterday, but afterwards I discover the film dates from the 1930s. "They risked their lives for a dollar a day," he says, as if he were there—and he is right. Epic stories are always contemporary, but I shall only come to understand this later, when I watch the film. "I'll show you where they did the filming," he says. "It isn't far, this is only a small island, it's only twelve miles long." At the end of the track the van can go no further. From there we can see the two tiny islands that lie off the most westerly point: Oileán Dá Bhranóg and An tOileán Iartbach. The lighthouse is situated on the second one. "It works automatically. But there used to be a lighthouse keeper who was sometimes unable to get off the island for weeks at a time because the sea was so dangerous." He points to a boiling mass of white surf just off the coast. A small stone pier juts out into the sea. "The wrong spot, of course, and totally useless. Built by an engineer from Dublin who knew better than the fishermen. When the weather's bad there's no way a *curragh* can get through that!"

I want to get nearer, but he stays sitting in the van. I try to imagine one of those tiny, tarred, fragile-looking, flimsy boats in a surf like this, and later on that day I see the reality, for though it was only a film, the men, the boat, and the surf were real enough, and they fought for their lives and for that single dollar. A raging sea, the three men outlined against the white spume like daguerre-otypes, tossed up, plunged down, vanishing behind walls of water; how they managed to film it is a mystery to me. Now I understood Angus thinking he was there, for here in this land of storytellers the tale must have been told hundreds of times, and they still had the images to prove it. The only one who has forgotten it all is the sea itself, which has nothing to do but hurl itself repeatedly against these same rocks in a hypnotic, eternal rhythm. Borges once said that in order to imagine eternity one should think of an angel stroking his wing across a block of marble until it has disappeared altogether.

I watch the water lunge at the rocks, fall back and attack again with deepest ash gray and black that detonates into white against the stone. A piece of seaweed the length of a child's arm washes up on to the quay as if someone has thrown it to me. I pick it up, *long rods, sea rods*, it's hollow, the stalk of a plant from the world of water. "Ten pounds a ton we used to make," Angus says. "We went about bent double under that stuff, can you imagine it?"

We drive back along the narrow main road. He points to a minuscule, decrepit house off to the right. "That's where the mapmaker used to live," he says, "the *Fear na Mapaí*. An Englishman, true, but he's written the best book about the island. Or so they say, I mean I can't read it. But that's what people say. I knew him too, you'd see him all over the place in the oddest spots, and he was always sounding out everyone. He stayed here for twelve years. Always drawing. They still sell his maps. He wanted to hear all the stories, especially the old people's. An Englishman, imagine! Us lads would be perched up on the cliff fishing, say three hundred feet above the sea, not many knew that spot and it was dangerous to boot, you couldn't see from up there what was happening down below, a rope with a hook on it, you just felt when you had a bite, then it was all down to hauling the fish up and trying to stop the gulls devouring it before you had hold of it. We used to sit on a really narrow ledge, I'd never dare do it now. But there he would be—he always wanted to know the name of everything for his map."

I still have to see the seven churches. Na Seacht dTeampaill. While Angus remains within the shelter of his van I wade through soaking wet grass between the graves with their Celtic crosses and runes. Seven turns out to be just two, with clouds for a roof, so that I receive an unrelenting christening. It is said that Latin monks are buried here and, who knows, perhaps they are.

On an island where Aristotle (*Harai Steatail*) still figures in popular legend, and where by the fifth century the venerable Enda was to be found discussing with the venerable Colm the grave of the Abbot of Jerusalem, who was supposed to have lived there for about 350 years, it all becomes such a wondrous tale of a thousand-and-something nights that, standing in the museum the same afternoon and reading about the riddles thrown up by reality, I am not in the least bit surprised by any of it.

Of course, Ireland was attached to America and Scandinavia for a thousand million years, and naturally, once the island had been formed, the rainwater made tiny fissures in the surface of the limestone that later became deep grooves, and who would deny that the sea has sculpted rocks a hundred meters high by repeatedly crashing against them, rocks of which, should the islanders ever disappear, all that will remain is a reef which would pose a danger to passing ships, should there still be shipping. Everything is true here, and if you do not believe it you have only to look at the photographs in which Time the magician demonstrates his art; fossilized remains of coral and shells from the ancient tropical sea that used to swell where I am presently so cold, tiny sea creatures who fell into the warm mud of the seabed and were compressed into limestone, sludge that sucked in the larger shellfish and, with the sea's help, turned them into a petrified treasure chamber. The rocks and crevices, I notice them on the cover of the book Angus was talking about by that man from England. A black-and-white photograph shows the stones seared and shiny in the rain, bisected by vertical and horizontal scours of weather-beaten rock. I buy the book and read it in my pink nursery, while the elements tug and tear at the windowpane.

A few hours later, when I have been out to find something to eat and have walked back with the whiskey leprechaun perched on my shoulder, my landlady puts on the video of *Man of Aran* for me. The men in their boat and the black-clad women dragging the heavy stalks of hollow seaweed up on land in baskets, the cry that goes up in the village when after many days the men catch a shark, and like a scene from an Eisenstein film you see them on the move, men, women and children with faces which they now no longer have. They lug the huge iron cooking pot to the jetty where the gigantic liver is to be cooked. Nine hundred liters of oil will melt from it to become flickering lights in all those little houses: a miracle.

Seaweed becomes kelp, shell becomes stone, liver becomes light, earth becomes turf, and rocks and sea-wrack become soil in which to grow potatoes. I am looking in on a world that just a minute before turned a corner in time for good, but which has left its memories among the never-changing decors of stone and water.

"Gone, vanished," wrote the Dutch poet Gerrit Kouwenaar, in a line of harsh irrevocability which was designed to stem the passing of time and disappearance of the known world—something that can never work unless a miracle occurs, and in this case the miracle is the book I have purchased that afternoon. I go on reading the first volume of Tim Robinson's *Stones of Aran* until deep into the night. The title of this first volume is *Pilgrimage*, the second *Labyrinth*, and in the stillness of the night, which is accentuated rather than reduced by the sound of the storm outside, the island on which I find myself is created for a second time, but this time from words. I do not believe there is another book in the world like it. In this first volume it is as if every meter of the coast, with its types of stone, plants, birds, stories, names and shapes has been described. The map at the back of the book was drawn by the writer himself; the route he took starts at the easternmost point, continues on past the high cliffs of the southern coast to An tOileán Iartach, the most westerly point, and then back by way of the north coast. In doing so he has achieved the impossible; by taking a geographical reality, describing it so meticulously and embedding it in a past of folk tales, legends, and history he has thwarted the transience of at least one small part of the globe. As storyteller, cartographer, geologist, botanist, detective, and meteorologist, he has physically permeated the present and psychologically the past, like a latter-day Stanley in some kind of mythical Africa. The second volume describes the interior of the island and once again you get the feeling that every stone has been upturned, every document read, every sound listened to, as though the walls of time do not exist. This second part is called *Labyrinth* not only because on twenty-eight hectares as many as forty fields can lie between the stone walls and these can be owned by five different farmers, but also because the author seems to have slipped through the mesh of time's net in order to put the unbelievable convolutions of human society in such a small area under a microscope. The result is a classic work. Admiration always contains an element of inquisitive jealousy. You know you could never do something like it yourself, if only because such a project would bind you to a single isolated spot for at least part of your life.

TWO YEARS LATER when I visit Inishmore a second time, I call on the author, in his house on the Irish coast at Roundstone, a small harbor in Connemara more or less opposite the islands. It is as though he still wants to keep an eye on them. He receives me in a sober room with a large window that looks out at the sea, so that it seems as if the sea wants to come in as well. He is sober-looking too, there's something monkish and military about him, extremely English, with a reservoir of humor that remains closed for the time being. That comes to the fore only later, when his wife, Máiréad, joins us and we eat and drink and look at his paintings. Downstairs is the office of his small literary publishing company, and his studio containing the thirteen-volume diary of twelve years on Aran, a bulging card index and all the reference material. He wrote the second volume here, "too far from the island," as he says on the first page, "to touch it, too near for Proustian telescopy." I say that when I read it I nevertheless often thought of Proust, especially the final part of *A la recherche du temps perdu*, where the writer talks about the enormous position people take up in time compared to their minor position in space, and he laughs and tells me that during those twelve harsh years on the island he read out loud all four thousand pages of Proust to his wife, first in English, then in French.

How came he to be on Aran? Pure chance. And that chance became a detour which has lasted twenty-five years. A mathematician by training he was living as a painter in London. "I'd just turned thirty and we simply went there as visitors. Back then it was all extremely primitive. In the house we rented there was a sack full of earth with a stone on top of it to put against the door so as to keep the wind from blowing it down. We had to learn to bake our own bread, and we were only accepted once we had made our own small field to grow potatoes in. All we had were ourselves and the books, and my work. I went through all those circles of heaven and hell, learned Gaelic, otherwise it would have been totally pointless. This was all back in 1972. I made the map because it was sometimes very difficult to find the way in that labyrinth of thousands of small walls. Somebody at the post office had said: "Well, why don't you make a map?" It had never occurred to me, except as a metaphor in one of my paintings." In the hall leading to his studio the original covers practically the whole wall, I recognize it from reproductions in books.

"I'm rather proud of it, it still sells."

Later on over dinner I sit below one of his paintings, an undulating, geometric image in white and pale blue, aesthetic and pure, strict, yet not so strict, like the man himself. While his wife is speaking, he remains silent, only occasionally filling in small details. "After our first sleepless, ice-cold night in that tiny house we sat on the edge of the bed with our backs to one another weeping into our teacups and moaned; what had we done!" The image which forms is one of shared adventure, of something small which began almost by accident and grew into an overwhelming passion, hilarious and lonely, overpowering. His Proust matched by her Virgil and Dante, two people reading to one another on long winter nights, a monastery for two in which slowly throughout all those years the Book is created from the stories of the people of the island, from observations and reading and time and time again from, as he puts it, the complexity of the ground below each step you take, the history of the earth under your feet, what it consists of, what has taken place upon it, what grows on it, what flies over it, who lives off it. He must have taken hundreds of thousands of steps in those twelve years. Steps that have been transmuted into words that have preserved at least one small piece of the world in all its completeness.

The following day, I return to the island, simultaneously in a book and in the real world. And once again a storm is raging over the sea. The man who clips my ticket for the boat is the same one as two years previously, someone who could have played Death in the Bergman film *The Seventh Seal*. He is reading a book by Bruce Chatwin. When I wake the following morning the weather is fine. Cold and wintry, but so piercingly bright and clear that it hurts your eyes. Tim Robinson said that whatever I do I must visit the "wormhole," Poll na bPéist. I start to walk there along the stony beach under the steep cliff, but the sea is too wild. I turn back and climb to the top. There is no path and I follow the cliff edge until I get there. Deep below, the water boils in a black rectangle which it is difficult to believe is not man-made. Under the rocks, only a few metres from the surf, there is a tiny opening that invisibly connects the basin of the rectangle with the ocean. Daredevils have been known to swim through this wormhole, but it is supposed to be exceptionally perilous. The sea puffs and thrusts through the narrow hole, while crashing over it at the same time, a wild and tenacious swell that causes the maddened white foam in the black rectangle to spurt furiously upwards. Nature as theater, unaffected by our presence. And I am reminded of what Tim Robinson said to me: "Nature knows nothing about us and takes no notice of us. One should forgo these overluxuriant metaphors that covertly impute a desire of communication to nonhuman reality. We ourselves are the only source of meaning, at least on this little beach of the universe. These inscriptions that we insist on finding on every stone, every sand-grain, are in our own hand. . . . We are writing a work so vast, so multivocal, so driven asunder by its project of becoming coextensive with reality, that when we come across scattered phrases of it we fail to recognize them as our own."

2000

Nooteboom's Hotel 1

A STORY ABOUT HOTELS can, of course, be written only in a hotel. A hotel is a closed world, a demarcated territory, a *claustrum*, a place one enters freely. The guests are not there by chance, they are members of an order. Their room, whether simple or luxurious, is their cell. When they shut the door of that room behind them and are *within*, they have withdrawn from the world.

The hotel in which hotels are going to be written about must be carefully selected. I have chosen the Ritz in Barcelona, but it could have been Brown's in London, Santa Luzia in Viano do Castelo, Reid's on Madeira, Hofman in Bandung or the Albergo Nazionale in Rome. What they have in common, which appeals to me, is their air of bygone times. An old-fashioned type of tap that doesn't always work, a hall porter you would like to have had as your father, colors that are no longer in vogue, the paint peeling here and there, a surfeit of mirrors, hairline cracks in the porcelain, the wear and tear of hundreds of thousands of disappeared shoes in the weave of the carpets, a lift which momentarily, but decidedly, hesitates before ascending, a room which by its tranquillity banishes all thought of other rooms.

The room in which I am staying at present, number 523, is decorated in the palest Greenland green. Sometimes I think that all the room numbers of all the hotels I have ever stayed in, added together, contain a coded message about my destiny and my persona, but I will never discover that cabbalistic number, which really must exist, because I have not kept a record of the numbers. Doubting Thomas.

For someone who may well spend months of any one year in hotels, I have a fatal character flaw: I am afraid of hotel fires. I do not know exactly when it started, although I do remember pictures of a hotel fire in Tokyo. Plummeting bodies, waving people not meaning to greet anyone, curtains billowing, tied-together sheets pointing to an abyss, clouds of smoke. Two years ago I missed the big conflagration at the Corona de Aragón in Zaragoza by one day. Franco's widow was rescued, a number of officers remained lying in the swimming pool up on the roof until the helicopters arrived, but there were eighty-one dead. The Spanish papers were full of scorched photographs, and they sometimes still appear in my nightmares. Hotel fires catch my eye in newspapers in the same way someone who is afraid of flying notices an air disaster before any other news, as confirmation of the rationality of his fear. But there are reassuring statistics for flying, whereas there are none for hotel fires. Even so, I do not go as far as one of my friends, who always has with him a good length of knotted rope and an iron hook. *Amor fati.*

The cause of the fire in Zaragoza was a pan catching fire while *churros*—elongated doughnuts Spaniards enjoy with their breakfast—were being fried. I find the thought that my fate might depend upon them most displeasing, which is why the first thing I always do is read the safety regulations. The Ritz's are reassuring, if only because they are printed in Catalan, a language I do not speak but can read. Because of this, the fire instructions have something of the palimpsest about them, an exhortation in

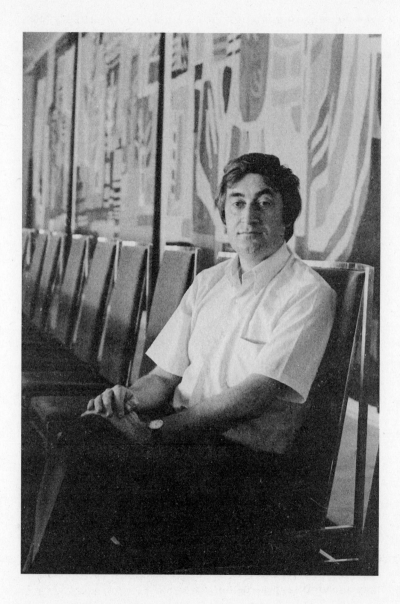

a defunct language; it is as if the eventual fire to which they refer may once have taken place in the Kingdom of Middle Earth, not here, not now. At any rate, there is no longer any need for me to fear it. "*Non perdeu la serenitat,*" it says—"Do not lose your serenity." It seems that not only are guests of the Ritz expected to possess this quality of nature, but also to hold on to it once they discover that a fire has started. All right. "*No correu, ni crideu*"—"Do not shout, do not run." Silent, composed, calm of gait, I remove myself from where the fire has started. "*Si es cala foc a la vostra roba, estireu-vos a terra I rodoleu.*" Here the advice is a little less restrained: "If your clothes catch fire: stop, drop, and roll." Stop, drop, rock and roll. "*En cas de molt fum, gategeu.*" I had to think about that one. "In the event of heavy smoke, *gategeu?*" Substitute a *c* for the *g*, leave out the rest and there you have it: crawl like a cat, *on all fours*. How one is supposed to open the door it does not say, but perhaps you are not meant to, just calmly and stoically await your inevitable fate. *Ecrivain fumé au Ritz* (Smoked Writer *au Ritz*).

Looking around, it is clear there are worse places to die. The carpet is the color of rusty iron. To the left of the bed there is a large faded cupboard with a man-sized mirror attached to one door. Both doors open toward the bed. One can therefore view oneself reclining in splendid isolation or, should the occasion present itself, with company as a *tableau vivant érotique*. The Ritz leaves this up to its guests. One can of course simply leave the doors closed. Nevertheless, this door concerns me. Is it me who is perverse, or those who, in Edwardian times, designed it so that it opened? I would estimate that more than fifty thousand people have occupied this room since the hotel was built. Statistically speaking, then, this mirror must have reflected a thing or two, but it remains silent as the earth into which so many of those guests have already disappeared.

The central heating was made by the Guitart company. The radiator is four-lobed and I would think it dates from about 1912. It probably makes a ticking noise in winter. The air conditioning is less ancient, but pretty old nonetheless. When I turn it on it drones like a DC-3, then settles down and imitates the faraway chugging of an ocean liner. Half asleep, I think I am on board a ship, but where is it heading?

The waste-paper basket is the first genuine anachronism. It is made of bronze-colored plastic. I do not like it, so I do not give it anything. By contrast, the furniture handles and fastenings are copper. In the hall to the bathroom there is a tiny door that comes up only as far as my hips. On opening it, I see the hotel's innards: gurgling pipes, sighs and hisses from the underworld, and intriguingly enough, my downstairs neighbor's roll of toilet paper.

The lamp serves as a reminder that writing is easier than describing. Emerging from a rosette-like metal plate of which I do not know the correct name, it hangs from the ceiling on three cords, like an upturned illuminated vase. The three cords, I shall keep calling them that, are attached to a band of ribbed metal, decorated with bows and other apparently meaningless orna-ments. Still, someone thought it all up, and not only that, *designed* it too. Who? Is he dead by now? Bound to be. One of the anony-mous dead, living on in a lamp. A curiously stylized fruit hangs underneath in a ring of twelve triangles (yes, twelve—a grown man actually got out of bed to count them).

BAR, BED, BANISTERS, bath. To the right of the bed, beside the oval lamp with its copper base, the telephone. Pale, beige, plastic. And blind, for it sports no numbers. If you pick it up, it swallows briefly. This is followed by a vague, oceanic murmuring, and, if you are lucky, a Spanish voice that says *"Dígame!"*—"Tell me!" Tell me what? Something which in Spain is a normal expression when you pick up the phone, to me expresses the fundamental nature of hotels. Of course, there are hotels with and hotels without a telephone in the room, and there are hotels where no one answers, or where the thing does not work, but what is fundamental about staying in a hotel, the quintessence, is that you can ask "them" (that is to say: the others) something, whereas "they" cannot ask you. At the other end of that telephone there is water, food, manpower, knowledge. Not one of those invisible individuals posted at the other end would ever take it into his head to telephone *me* and ask me to polish his shoes, bring her a Scotch or mineral water, arrange tickets for the opera, put a call through to Athens for him. But I *do* have the right to do all this, I purchased it when I bought the right to stay in room 523 for the night. Sometimes they get their own back, at five thirty in the morning, because I have asked them to, having a plane to catch at some unholy hour. From the depths of slumber there is that momentary feeling of panic, a hand gropes toward the unnerving sound, and then the voice of someone who has been up far longer, announcing not without a certain perfidy, "Good morning! It's half past five!" There are worse scenarios: when the owner of that cheerful voice makes a mistake and though the message is correct (it *is* five thirty), it was not meant for you.

WHO POPULATES these hotels, besides people traveling for their pleasure? Politicians, civil servants, chess players, salespeople, reps, musicians, bankers, journalists. That is by no means all, but those are the main categories. What they have in common is that, generally speaking, they are not on their own at home, whereas in a hotel they are. This is either resolved with a newspaper, with a book, with alcohol, by chance or prearranged (and prepaid) meetings, or remains unresolved. I have lost count of how many hotels I have stayed in. The Dutch photographer, Eddy Posthuma de Boer, with whom I have made many journeys, keeps notes: who, where, when, which room number. When the NRC Handelsblad asked me to put together a hotel, made up of all the hotels I had ever been to, or rather, of the qualities that most appealed to me in each one, I demurred, saying it would be an exercise in snobbery, because in constructing the ideal hotel, you leave out all the bad bits. And besides, the thing would be bigger than Birmingham: I am forty-eight, after all, and have been traveling for half a lifetime. None of this was a problem.

So I set off down the long staircase toward the shadows of my memory, and it turned out to be just that: shadowy. A maze of rooms with numbers on them; rooms where it is snowing beyond the window panes but where I am still strolling around in tropical gear; balconies that do not belong on the façade; corridors with illegible notices; lounges with a lowland plain on one side and high mountains on the other; friendly Asian waiters and frozen rivers; lifts that end on the roof; chaos. In order to have something to hold on to in this labyrinth, I asked Posthuma de Boer to let me have a list of the hotels we had stayed in together. He sent the following inventory: Sucre Palace Hotel, La Paz; Grand Hotel Bamako, Mali; Motel Sevaré, Mopti; Terminus, Niamey, Niger; Los Almohades, Agadir; Hotel Salam, Taroudannt; Hotel du Sud, Tinerhir; Hotel Mamounia, Marrakech; Hotel Boumian, Les Saintes-Maries de la Mer; Hotel Jules César, Arles; Hotel Semiramis, Puerto de la Cruz; Hotel Mencey, Santa Cruz de Tenerife; Arrecife Grand Hotel, Arrecife, Lanzarote; Hotel Victoria, Madrid; Hotel Cruzeiro, Bragança; Atlantic Hotel, Banjul, Gambia; Apollo Hotel, Banjul, Gambia; Palmeras Playa, Tenerife; Hotel Mayantigo, Santa

Cruz de la Palma; Pacific Hotel, Tokyo; Royal Hotel, Osaka; Hagi Grand Hotel, Hagi; Traveller's Inn Hotel, Anchorage, Alaska; and the Dai-Ichi Shimbasi Hotel, Tokyo. But now I come to type out this litany of lost days, I discover that he is not infallible either, for where are Lima, Brasilia, Bahia de San Salvador, where is the Copacabana in Rio, the Tusculum in Berlin, the Michelet-Odéon in Paris? And what about the Eastern & Oriental in Penang, the now anonymous building in Malacca where we sought out the graves of the East India Company's forefathers; and where is that trashy hotel, the Hyatt in Kuala Lumpur, and the idiotic, dispro-portionately large rooms of the Raffles in Singapore, where the *kipahs* on the ceilings swirl the heat around as if there are single-engine aircraft on the floor above, pointed directly downwards?

ALL RIGHT: the ideal hotel, Nooteboom's Hotel, 1 Paradise Parade, Shangri-La, Ultima Thule, next door to the Restaurant Chez God. Reclining chairs on Elysian lawns in Allah's garden, polar ice tinkling in glasses of nectar, buddhas underneath the holy bread-fruit trees, vestal virgins with stuffed pigeons on embossed plat-ters by Erté, and all of it cloaked in galactic silence. Something like this? Perhaps it would be better, after all, to begin with the reverse: with what I do *not* want. Not the murmurings of the fellow in the next room, nor the traces of someone else's lust or sounds of same, not the rooms where someone has probably committed suicide, nor the slow torture of the *gutta cadenda* from a leaky tap and the axiomatic certainty that the next drip is on its way, and the next, and the next. I do *not* want any of that. Do not want the masseuse in Bangkok who knocks on the door at the incorrect time and says, "Sir, you speak me come?" Not the temptation of the fridge containing the wrong beer and the right whisky. Not the sound of the vacuum cleaner in the hallway that reminds

one of *work*. Not the morning light whose laser beam pierces the
Freudian province where I am presently sojourning, it still being
nighttime for me. Not the conversation between two middle-aged
female voices, in a dialect straight out of *Finnegans Wake*, in which
I am ridiculed because I am still in bed. No television. No television? Call yourself a journalist? No television! And all those nights
in motels in Nevada or Arizona, when you . . . NO TELEVISION!
Solitude, silence, meditation, sleep. That is what I have paid for.

*   *   *

WHERE DOES A hotel's territory begin? Here at the Ritz the terri-
torial waters extend as far as the hall porter can see. He looks
good, his suit well-cut *café au lait*, elegant un-German peaked cap,
waistcoat, white bow tie. His gaze reaches right along the Gran
Via and the Calle Roger de Lluria, and plucks taxis from the traffic.
Lesser gods have need of a whistle. Whistles go with top hats, at
the Palmer House in Chicago or the Carlton Ritz in Montreal. No
whistles or fancy dress, they belong to football. I would sooner
take a room in a guest house. The true hall porter winks, the *ultimate* hall porter bats an eyelid. And I repeat, the genuine traveler
simply wants to sleep. The rest is *circumstance*, and anything left
after that is *pomp*. *Pomp* is what takes place when someone else is
footing the hotel bill. You, dear reader, have paid for this lounge
where I now sit beneath a blackened "Flora" from the pastoral days
of Marie Antoinette, flanked by two palms, gazing out across a
Persian carpet lawn on which neat beds of Bordeaux-red chairs
are arranged, in the style of a Louis who never existed. Fragile old
ladies sit staring drowsily into space.

I shut myself off from all this and build my own hotel. It
stands on four continents and in five seasons. I am keeping this
hall porter, but he will get a shock if he glances over his shoulder,

because he will see the lounge of the Royal Grove Hotel in Waikiki, Honolulu. That hotel is run by the Fong family, and its members are either to be found seated at the reception desk, or in the tiny grocer's shop next door, selling the tins of corned beef, which I prepare on my single-burner gas stove in room 26. But I am only taking the lounge, just so it will feel like coming home of an evening. "Good evelin, Mistel Nutbum." My room comes from Bali, except it is not a room, but a hut. Although it is on the ground floor I have to go up a staircase to get to it, a staircase for aristocratic Spanish feet (I have a pair for the occasion), the staircase from the Hotel de los Reyes Católicos in Santiago de Compostela. Are you still with me? We have climbed to the top, a gust of Galician autumn wind swirling about us, and have now arrived at ground level in Bali, at the Lechian Beach Hotel, Kuta. I can hear the sound of the gecko outside and am glad because I know he brings good fortune. It is hot, the fan is driven by buffalo, and in the distance I can hear the roar of the surf. In the middle of the night I get up and look outside, as I always do. Not to see where I am, but to make sure the world exists—and ergo, that I do too. Something for which an earlier generation of hotels needed walls of mirrors. Stay with me—even though it is a mite strange: we are looking at night-time Manhattan, and part of the harbor of New York, with the Statue of Liberty. We are in Brooklyn, on the eighth floor of the Bossert Hotel. Opposite us the impregnable battle lines of skyscrapers, illuminated. Nothing moves. A vision of the apocalypse: the neutron bomb has been dropped, but the dead have forgotten to turn out the lights before dying. *This was once a Dutch enclave.* It is all our fault. This is where Mammon lives, and he has written his memento mori in those empty towers. I bury myself under the sheets, wait for morning to come, and take the Bristol in Paris's lift down. Which just proves how fallible I am, because it is a heavenly lift, meant only for ascending to and arriving at a spot one will never again want to leave. But I have already reached the ground floor, and step out of the *belle époque* into the tropical, morning scent of the garden of the Village N'Gor Hotel in Dakar. Here is the ocean once more, a different yet identical one. Night has vanished with its swift hearse, leaving behind tears on the broad palm leaves. In a little while the sun will thrust its knife deep into them, but I will be long gone by then, breakfasting in the spacious dining room of the Parador Nacional de la Concordia in Alcañiz. The medieval hall of the fortified castle is empty. It is winter and snowing in this northern part of Spain. I am the only guest, and am sitting beneath the standard of Don Alonso de Aragón y de Foix. Coffee, *churros*, hard sweet biscuits. How is this monster I have constructed shaping up? A big hall that leads to the Fong family's living room, a room floating high above the cantilevers, a lift that goes nowhere. Not I, but the great Italian architect Barbieri should have designed this building: someone who does not write, but one who builds. What shall I do with the drawing room of the Infante do Sagres in Porto? Where will my guests eat *Sachertorte*, where will they have their nightcap if the bar of the Amstel Hotel in Amsterdam cannot be fitted in? And, by the way, where is my façade? I muse on all this as I munch my *churro*—and then from far away I hear the call of my lonely suitcase. Heading toward the sound I arrive at where I was already, room 523. It is high-ceilinged, this room, pale green, hushed. On the gleaming table stands my typewriter, and together we do what we always do in places like this—we write a story for other people.

SEPTEMBER 1981

At the Edge of the Sahara

WHEN I WAS ABOUT six years old, in front of our house in Rijswijk in Holland, there was a piece of waste ground that I called "The Land." A mysterious place. Tall plants which nowadays only come up to my waist made it seem like a jungle, and I can picture it even now: a dangerous place that I filled with my fears and fantasies.

I am often asked why I travel so much. I think it is because the world has now become "The Land." The fears have gradually become divided equally between home and elsewhere, but have acquired, shall we say, a mechanical quality along the way. So they are no longer of interest except as a means of wasting energy. The fantasies, the flights of imagination are galvanized by traveling, especially at that point where the visible cannot be readily defined. The aversion to living among the indescribable is what made me learn languages. I cannot imagine being in Spain or Peru without being able to speak to people there or read the papers. There are still enough riddles left over. But it was only later, during my trips to Africa, and now again at the northern edge of the Sahara, that I became aware of the excitement of being foreign.

The same old sense of excitement. Seeing things you do not understand, signs you cannot read, a language you cannot fathom, a religion you do not have any real conception of, a landscape that rebuffs you, lives you could not share. Something I count a blessing nowadays. The shock of the wholly unknown is one of gentle sensuality. If you are unable to join in there is a lot you can dispense with. Your masks do not count. As far as a Berber from Goulimine is concerned you could as easily be from Ohio, so that many of the nuances one has taken pains to cultivate no longer apply. And that makes this type of travel a pleasant sort of void, a state of zero-gravity in which, although the self does not lose all significance, a good deal does get written off—you float through those foreign climes, seeing, looking, watching, scratching the invulnerable surface here and there, and then you disappear again, returning emptier.

Spain used to give me that sensation. But through learning the language and a certain gift for mimicry my Spanish pleasure has turned into something else: in Spain I can pose as a Spaniard, slip into the enchantment of temporarily being something else, someone reading the local newspaper at a pavement café in Córdoba, which is also a vanishing act of sorts, and that is what it is about after all. Like reading the *Nice-Matin* in Cannes and melting into the tarmac of the Croisette, or the *Corriere della Sera* while you sit around in Catania's main square for three hundred or six thousand years.

Morocco is different. It is the superlative, the dizzy heights. True, it does mean being labeled a foreign idiot, but in accordance with the rules of reciprocity I do not get any further than "mysterious Berber" or "Arab clad in long robes" either, thus attaining a degree of invisibility into which "the seen" promptly disappears. For what I see, the little that I am capable of seeing, is in fact something other than what I see, just as what I hear is not information, only language that I cannot understand, whereas this is precisely its purpose: that it should be understood.

You are there and you are not there, and that is how I traveled through Morocco a second time. However, my journey commences at a place where none of the above applies; in a hotel straight out of a travel brochure, run from behind the scenes by silent, efficient Swiss. Where European bodies wallow in the warm November sun and tumble into the unreal blue water of the swimming pool, idling the time away like an arrogant, exclusive clan, waited upon by darting Moroccans who, deprived of their traditional robes for efficiency's sake, resemble the skinny, fleet-footed Spanish and Italian waiters the superior Northern European has already learned to tolerate in his own restaurants. All this breathtaking international contact causes the waiters themselves to feel vastly superior to their own village, tribe, and background; they have taken their first steps in the shadow-play of progress, the worm is in the apple, and every country has a right to its own rotten apple.

WHAT I REMEMBER most about the journey to Goulimine, in the deep south, are the boys with the squirrels. All of a sudden up in the hills at a bend in the road there they are, their young boys' bodies blending into the landscape like something entirely natural, as if they grew there too. They are holding aloft a moving object. When I pull up, it turns out to be a squirrel, which they have captured and are trying to sell. The creature has a rope around its neck and hangs in the air like a character from the Arabian alphabet, fashioned in fur, long tail tucked in under it as far as possible, eyes darting back and forth in terror. Later, in the Atlas Mountains, I watch a battered old Volkswagen pull up next to a couple of lads like these. A blonde girl gets out and goes over to the boys. When she sees what it is they are selling she remains stock-still for a moment, and then proceeds to throw up against the stony mountainside. The boys laugh because they do not know what else to do.

Goulimine, city of blue men. Nearing it at last I feel a touch of excitement. Why? It will be just like Timbuktu or Zagora, places where the men emerge from the desert and disappear into it again. No different to what I already know. I think it is the extremity of the surrounding landscape, the exceptional nature of the lives lived here, just as a place of this sort forms a literal exception to the surrounding void. Although here, too, tourism is making increasing inroads. No longer is feasting upon the exceptional and different a privilege reserved for the writer. Amid the inconceivable otherness and authenticity, there now lurks the all too conceivable artificial and fake, American whining, and the hawking of pathetic artifacts.

But the camel market itself is not for our benefit. It is as though the very clouds have left a space above the square. Open, dusty and all but empty, it is full of dung and loose stones. A few ailing eucalyptus trees surround it—a poignant effort foundering on the hot sun of two o'clock in the afternoon. Bellowing camels change hands, front and back legs bound together, men in djellabas make vicious test runs on scrawny mules, kicking and wheeling sharply. Two splendid black enigmas, hooded and veiled, with yellow plastic shoes below their darkness, sit against a wall in the dust and hold a conversation beneath their swathes of cloth. Over in a corner grain is being purchased (WHEAT FURNISHED BY THE PEOPLE OF THE USA, NOT TO BE SOLD).

There is nothing more after Goulimine, the red road on the map passes through a completely white area until Tan-Tan, but Tan-Tan has yet to amount to anything, although the first tourists have started arriving. Drawn to the emptiness on the map, I drive along this road for a distance, and then turn off into the parched earth, skirting the dazzling white skeleton of a goat and coming to a standstill when a large train of camels passes by in complete silence. I promise myself that one day I will drive on, from Tan-Tan to Tarfaya, and after that to Aaiún, the Spanish Sahara, and Mauritania, but for now I turn and drive back toward the north.

IT IS DARK BY the time I reach Taroudannt. Somber, defensive walls several meters thick, within which the town lies secure. Not like in Avignon, where the town has burst through its walls and simply continued on the other side—so that the walls have something superfluous and therefore ridiculous about them—no, very much within, a space for people carved out of the rest of the world, a safe stronghold. The hotel is a midget arabic palace with few concessions to Western taste. An oriental, somewhat anointed feeling takes hold of me; I walk a little slower, shuffling slightly, and below the hibiscuses I drink a glass of tea in the moonlight, beside the tiled stream. An owl calls from somewhere among the trees, someone tells me it is a white one, a wistful little call as if he is unburdening himself to the moon about some minor matter or other of Arabian owl-anguish.

The following morning the cries are louder. As early as 5 AM, Allah's cockerel begins to crow, so noisily that I wake with a start; an endless exhortation to prayer, a voice whose interminable, shrieking turns of phrase sound at once tortured and routine. There is no avoiding it, the day has begun and Allah demands to be worshipped. Half an hour later when the muezzin finally stops I drift off again into rather vague dreams, sans time or place.

The morning is cold and misty. I step outside and into the Bible. What little sun there is setting the ochre town walls alight. Past them go the boys with their sheep, mules laden with bunches of twigs, Berbers from the surrounding district with wares for market. The birds babble in the mandarin trees to the beat of the coppersmith's hammer. Men sift grain through their hands, inspecting it, horses are being shoed, a woman gives a piece of raw earthenware a brief lick, herbs are weighed and weighed again, with a weight as light as a feather, the snake-charmer already has an audience, and the camels' feet are laid out in neat rows at the butcher's. *Balek! Balek!* shouts the mule driver with his load of great blocks of glistening salt. I am seeing the world as it no longer is; meaty smells emanate from tall, tapering, earthenware pots among the glowing charcoal, women in long black clothes and wearing fantastic jewelry separate the wheat from the chaff.

Why do I feel so happy here? Perhaps it is the quiet, the only sounds being those of man and beast. The mules are all parked in one corner of the market. In a few years it will be mopeds, later still cars. But not yet. Perhaps, too, it is because of the fact

that everything is so visible: how it is all made. Blacksmiths, tanners, and bakers all congregate around this market, scribes and storytellers, beggars and butchers, a miniature cosmos, a world complete in itself, providing for and serving itself, a world that seems to makes sense.

With his eyes and voice alone, the storyteller has opened up a crater of fiction in the midst of the crowd. Those listening to him are utterly captivated. There is a dreadful innocence about their concentration. His voice murmurs, catches, races, shouts, dies away again, and they follow, nothing distracts them. Now that really is writing! I would like to sink into it all, or alternatively just be part of it. But I get no further than a glass of mint tea. As I walk back to the town gates through the endless warren of the kasbah I can still hear the drums behind me, and the high, meandering flute of the snake-charmer.

"RETURNING TO A PLACE where we once dwelt is entirely possible, but returning to a moment we once experienced is, alas, impossible." This is the final sentence in Dr. P.J. Zwart's book, *Het mysterie Tijd* (The Mystery of Time). I traveled through Morocco in 1960. I took the bus (an extremely uncomfortable method of transport in those days) from Marrakech up through the northern Atlas by way of Ouarzazate, to the last border post before Mauritania, the M'Hamid oasis in the Sahara, where the tiny River Drâa disappears beneath the sand and the sand itself, along with some of the camels and very few of the Berbers, embarks upon the long march to Timbuktu. It was a wonderful journey through high, wild mountains, and hot, which made the cow's head perched all day on the lap of the man next to me particularly trying, and it was mysterious too, due to the strange, high, Assyrian-style red and ochre forts, called *ksa*, along the route.

In those days I was unhampered by any knowledge of the Berbers, all I did was look. Now that I know more about them, as usual I know less: a mysterious people whose origins are unknown, tribes with names like Tachelheïr and Tamazirt, a language, *tifinar*, written in a cryptic alphabet that surely Borges alone would have been able to decipher. There are hundreds of theories about where these Imazirenians actually came from, who they were; were they around when Dido, Princess of Tyre, founded Carthage? Or were they the Gérulen who provided Hannibal with carmine and elephants? Or the Ethiopians referred to by Skylax of Carthage? Or the Lixites of Hamon? Or were they, as Malek Ibn Marahbet claims, "Himyaritic, Modéritic, Coptic, Amalekite tribes who migrated together from Syria to North Africa..."?

Ancient is the word that springs to mind; the language, the names, the indeterminate history, the forts, the desert, the stony ground, the valleys, a world still shrouded in a sheath of antiquity and consequently exerting an almost forbidden attraction. The centuries-old, fossilized Talmudic wisdom in the *mellahs* or Jewish quarters within the kasbah walls, cabbalistic riddles, stories handed down from the Bible exclusively by word of mouth, fossilized language, fossilized gestures, the shepherd's crook, the farmer's plough, the storyteller's voice, the smith's furnace, the authority of the parables.

I am standing in front of the kasbah at Taourirt. I stood here thirteen years ago, in 1960. An old man took me inside then, showed me the synagogue—a loamy cave glistening with gold—and in the blisteringly hot afternoon sun, revealed to me a secret garden where rushes waved softly in water and frogs croaked foolishly. He plucked roses from a bush with a sweeping gesture and squashed the petals into my hand. And when we emerged from the garden I saw a woman in a long, pale-colored robe, with eyes that sparkled

blackly and a rose that hung down over her forehead. It is all gone now, except the memory.

I wander through the confusing alleyways of sand, past endless mud walls that merge together, disappear, begin anew, but I do not find the garden again. The Jews have gone; either the synagogue no longer exists, or people do not want to point it out to me, and if I did see the woman I did not recognize her. I did see Death. Over in a dark corner where it is damp and cold, a pile of dirty rags lies moaning. For that is all I can make out in the dimness, the remnants of a human being, a bundle of garments that looks as though it could not possibly weigh more than a couple of pounds. Yet the voice whines and mumbles and weeps softly. Somebody, something is dying, something old and already practically faded away, a disembodied mouth, a soul laid down in a corner by its fellow men. I move toward it, the voice switches to a lisping and a rattling, but I still cannot make out a head, and then a woman appears who gestures to me to leave, such ignominy is not for the eyes of a foreigner.

TAOURIRT, TIZI'N' Taddeght, Inassine, El-Kelaâ-des-Mgouna, El Gournt, Bournalne, Imiter—the names of the places on the way to Tinerhir. Den Doolaard, the eminent Dutch writer and traveler, passed through here some forty years ago. This part of the world is still wild and deserted and I hope it will stay that way. These vistas are devoid of sensuality, there is nothing seductive or pleasant about them apart from the pleasure they give me, a kind of exercise. What will I meet up with? A jackal, an army truck, three women bent double under fantastic bundles of rushes they could not possibly have collected anywhere—but then they are not going anywhere either, so that makes a certain sense. There are trucks too, which oblige you to abandon the narrow road for the gritty verge, and sometimes groups of men on mules or camels. And then all of a sudden in a bend in the road, a goatherd. His goats are not grazing in the meadow, because there is no meadow; they are up aloft, among the branches of some hard, thorny trees. I stop to watch and we regard one another from a distance. It is a pretty bizarre scene: him with a crook and a dog and all his goats up a tree, me on an empty road in a world masquerading as a moonscape. Slowly he comes toward me, laughs with a mouth that boasts few teeth, and says something I do not understand. We smoke a cigarette together, and he taps the car and says, "France?" I reply, "No, Holland." And, oh God, a flash of tremendous yearning passes across his face, as though I have said "from paradise," and he says, "Moi, Hollande, travail?" Him, with his staff, his goats, and his long sinewy legs planted upon the ground, as if they themselves are made of stone. I feel a great sense of shame and do not know what to say, but it does not matter because he cannot understand me anyway, and so I leave him on his own and move on, a rapidly disappearing emissary from a longed-for world.

TINERHIR. FROM the terrace of the ruined palace of the former Pasha of Marrakech I watch the end of the day close like a ring around the end of the market. Down below on the big, open, dusty plain, white tents are pitched. Small fires are smoking everywhere. Men in long brown and white djellabas crowd around storytellers in large circles, their horses and mules abandoned to the open spaces in between. And stationed on the periphery of this whole cosmos are the big trucks, waiting to transport the Berbers back to their far-flung, out-of-the-way villages, way up in the petrified Atlas, above which the moon is now being raised like a mirror. I go down. It is quiet in the oasis. Drums in the distance and here murmuring water, rustling palms. It is almost unbearably romantic: pale moonlight shines on the earthen, ochre ruins and then upon a graveyard, ploughed furrow of the dead, simple shards sticking out of the ground, each one of them marking an anonymous death. Anyone would think I was Novalis, the way I am spooking around in the moonlight through the approaching night. It is getting chilly, it feels as if the mountains are rolling their own cold stony air down into the sheltered, sensual, secretive oasis.

At the marketplace the men sit by their fires, smoking and talking. The blacksmith, crouched in his dark cave, glares like an evil spirit with blazing eyes. The sparks fly around his ears, Jan Hanlo's angels swish back and forth on the sandy path and call out half shyly, half provocatively, *"Bonsoir."** The petroleum lamps in

---

* Jan Hanlo (1912–1969), Dutch poet.

the tiny shops are turned higher, a man picks up two camel's feet, inspects them under the dim lamp and puts them down again. A skinned and peeled cow's head is cleft in two; the eyes, dark and serious, are still in place and look almost as sorrowful as those of the King, although he is not sorrowful but vengeful and harsh.

Night falls early. There are hardly any guests in the hotel. I am served *tagine*, a dish in an earthenware pot, rice accompanied by a pigeon and some steamed prunes. It is 9 PM and the waiter wants to go home. Half an hour later everything is cold, deserted, and deathly quiet. From my room I can see two yellow lights making their lonely way through the valley—outside the oasis the bare nothingness begins. I watch the silhouette and its shadow; it appears to be snowing lightly above the plain of the Drâa, there is even a moon.

ELIAS CANETTI'S brilliant little book on Marrakech contains a gruesome passage, his description of a visit to the graveyard of the *mellah*. He gets literally pursued and cornered by an angry mob of the crippled, blind, and mad, an apocalyptic throng with outstretched hands, a tribe of beggars straight out of a Hieronymus Bosch painting.

Ten years later they are still there, but they do not move a muscle. Neither do they beg, just squat by the entrance, a demoralized assembly. The graveyard itself is a broad array of white tombs, a big white stone field surrounded by a wall, with the huge, riotous chocolate boxes of the rich up at the far end.

I am already halfway along when a man comes toward me, shouting. I do not understand him, but am aware he wants me to leave. This I am not willing to do, having been determined to see this very graveyard ever since reading Canetti. He shouts and threatens so I start shouting as well, two harmless loonies squaring up to one another at the hottest hour of the day, a pair of quacking ducks on death's dewpond. It lasts until his son arrives, informs me that his father is mad, curses him, and leads him away. After this I remain alone, until the son returns and tells me he and his father are virtually the only ones who still tend the graves, now that so many of the Jews have left.

I read the names, and he points to the graves of the great rabbis, tall, sculptured colossi ready to ascend unto heaven. It is extremely quiet. Beckoning, he coaxes me toward a low building where a strange little man in ritual attire, half blind, touches my face and asks me something. "Whether you have children," my guide explains. "No." The empty eyes take on a disappointed expression. He wants to lay his hand upon my head. Candles are lit, I have to bend down. Suddenly he is overflowing with magic incantations, they bubble up and pour forth over me, I am finally taking part in a rite of some sort again. I deposit some money in the copper pot being held up to me, receive a few more shoves, and return, thoroughly blessed, to the *mellah*.

Marrakech is not a city, it is an autonomous planet slung by divine providence, like a red whore (as a friend of mine put it), against the foothills of the Atlas, whose lofty snow-covered tops sparkle in the distance. It is a city to read about in a book that takes years to finish. The best thing is to immerse yourself in it, letting yourself fall through all the trapdoors of its wild and bewildering history, allowing yourself to be taken by the hand and led to the graves of the Saadi, Almoravid, and Alouite dynasties, realizing you know nothing about Moroccan history, have precious little real grasp of Islam either, and what an idiotic state of affairs this is. And then to shrug off your guilty conscience about this in the perpetual riot of the Djeema el Fnaa, or lament quietly beneath the jasmine trees.

The hippies, who have also discovered the place, are right; *this is where it's at*, the only planet to be on—here among the fairy tales and the snakes, the weavers, tanners, and coppersmiths. Not in the cold, materialistic north, with the bare obscenity of Amsterdam's Dam Square as its zenith, but here, drawing up a chair under the carbide lamps on the main square—where for a few dinars you can sup with the populace and contemplate your navel until you have examined the entire contents of your skull. "Life and death, why, they are brothers," pronounces the white-slippered keeper of the Medersa ben Yussef. His long brown hands stroke the marble heraldic eagles on a kind of baptismal font, commissioned in the tenth century by—and reverently he recites the names within the name—Abd el Malek Ben El Mansour Abi Amir. We walk through the Medersa together and are suddenly pitched forward from our dark passageway onto a court into which the light of the heavens is presently being poured. All is embellishment, opulence, calligraphy, ornament. I ask him what the letters crawling meanderingly across the pink stones signify, and he tells me that what is written there comes from the Koran, and is a passage about death, and while he holds my hand and fixes his big black eyes on me with great intensity, that is what he says—quite casually, nonetheless—"Life and death, why, they are brothers. *C'est juste, le Koran, non?*"

"*Oui, c'est juste.*" And he entrusts me once more to the stony web.

1973

That Earlier War:
the Memorial in Canberra

SUNDAY APRIL 25, 1915. As long as the moon is up you can make out the vague shape of the land; a big fish, floating, deathly quiet, half out of the water. The ships at sea sail slowly, they steal along, cannot see one another. Homer once referred to a sea, a different one, as "wine-dark." Destroyers, troopships, old battlecruisers. On board, most of the Australian First Division. The four thousand men of the Third Brigade will go in first. They are billeted on the warships, which are less vulnerable to cannon fire than the troopships. The final stage will be completed in the rowing boats, now bobbing up and down in bunches behind the large vessels. The moon is due to go down at 3 AM, which is when it will all happen, in that irresolute hour between night and morning, hour of half-darkness, shadows, and ambiguity. The soldiers do not know whether the Turkish foe has noticed them. No light is visible on the vague land mass. The crew of the battle-ships have given the infantrymen the use of their quarters; in a while they will wake them with hot chocolate.

The Gallipoli offensive is to last for more than nine months. Of the Australians alone 7,500 men will die, 2,400 will be wounded, many scarred for life, blinded, lost. They are all volunteers, they hail from all six states of the Dominion, from the remotest corners of the outback, they will fight in the Middle East and in the muddy fields of France. Almost sixty thousand will not return. Their names are engraved in the wall of the war memorial in Canberra. Somebody once worked out how long it would take to walk past all those names, how many steps it would take. A lot of steps.

The expedition to Gallipoli will be a failure, will end in a retreat, the only consolation being that that retreat does not turn into a massacre. War is chess, but with people. The young Churchill is the grandmaster of the chessboard in London. Whoever gains the peninsula will be able to move unchallenged through the Dardanelles, the narrow passageway connecting the Aegean to the Black Sea, and to Russia. The Russians, at war with Germany and Turkey, have asked the British to relieve the Turkish pressure on Russian troops in the Caucasus. The Russians themselves have come to the aid of the French by invading eastern Prussia, with disastrous consequences. If the British now make a move toward Constantinople then the Turks will have to withdraw at least part of their army from the Russian front. The Gallipoli peninsula, lying opposite Turkish Asia, would seem to be the ideal place for such an offensive. The Dardanelles flows between the land masses as a narrow river, running into the Sea of Marmora, which in turn empties into the Black Sea. At the head of the Straits lies Cape Helles; Troy once lay on the other side. With ships alone it would be impossible, they would be too vulnerable to the weaponry of the Turkish troops on the peninsula. Peninsula, spit of land, craggy hills, stony ground. I see it later on old topographic maps: ravines, crests of hills, open plains. For the Allies it is to be a gruesome death trap, and ninety thousand Turks will perish too.

I have a book by the Australian military historian, C.E.W. Bean, which describes the agony, the tragedy, day by day.* It is

---

* C.E.W. Bean, ANZAC to Amiens.

a diary from hell. Courage, confusion, needless dying, lack of communications, mud, sickness. And that grandmaster of war, Churchill, had made it all sound so simple: "To bombard and take the Gallipoli Peninsula, with Constantinople as its object." In March and April, British and French warships had attacked the Dardanelles, only to be humiliatingly driven back. Now it was the turn of the army, and they too would meet with disaster. By January 1916 it was all over. Only the dead remained behind.

It is all there in the war memorial. The watch belonging to the sergeant from Queensland, which stopped that morning at seventeen minutes to five when he sprang from his boat into the water, in order to make land. It is as if time had wanted to burn itself into that object, the hour on the face will forever be the same, and this comes across as a denial, a refusal. The finest (a word perhaps best avoided) monuments are not those thought up afterward, but those that happened at the time: that watch, the landing craft peppered with bullet holes. You stand there staring dumbly at objects like these; disconnected from their own moment in time, they are no longer themselves, yet still are. A scale model affords me a bird's-eye view of the whole peninsula. It is covered in the markings and flags of the strategists. You can see that it is only a few miles wide, that the battle zone was never very big, and you cannot conceive that this miserable strip of land was worth more than a hundred thousand people dying for. It is accompanied by photographs and two dressmaker's dummies—soldiers with those typically Australian hats, leggings, clodhoppers: the khaki I remember so well from a different war. They are aiming their bayonets at something you cannot see, but you know those fights were fought with bayonet and knife, man to man, a ghastly way to do battle, to die. Entire battalions marched forward to be mowed down by the machine guns, and they knew it, and the officers who gave the orders, and who themselves perished in their hundreds, knew it too.

There is also a diorama of this battle, the attack on Lone Pine. Lonely Pine, war is always good for intentionally or unintentionally bizarre poetry. The land that lay there, its gullies, hill ranges, rises, and rifts all had their own Turkish names, bestowed by history, by farmers and fishermen. But wars also bequeath their own names, cynical, romantic, as if the horror can be kept in check by semantics. The Turks had dug themselves in by Lonely Pine; they covered their trenches with tree branches, mud and earth. In the distance the sea, blue, a battleship, fire everywhere, destiny, and in the foreground muddy men locked in close combat, the Australians with white patches sewn on their uniforms, so as to be able to recognize each other when everything had become unrecognizable through dust or sludge. A Kienholz* has been at work here. I stand frozen to the spot in front of it. Just as with the watch, nothing moves, the man who falls does so forever, his bayonet will always be pointing toward that other head, they will constantly die there, first one, then the other.

THERE IS SOMETHING exceptional about this museum: with all its blood and death, its aircraft, cannons, uniforms, medals, paintings of heroes and battles, it may at first sight seem to be romanticizing the military enterprise, but it is not, the effect is far too melancholy for this, the numbers too devastating. It is not just the First World War, but the Second World War too, *my* war. What do I know about it? I was not yet seven when it broke out. We lived near the airstrip at Ypenburg. Heinkels, Stukas, the shrieking sound of diving fighter planes, the dry splutter of anti-aircraft guns,

---

* Edward Kienholz (1927–94), American artist who made assemblages and environments with "real" objects, in which people were situated.

Rotterdam burning in the distance. A car containing German officers had strayed too far along the River Vliet, on the assumption that that section had already been captured. The car was fired on, and hit the water. I was there later, when they dredged up the bodies. It is not something you forget, the water that trickled from those strangely long, leather coats, their indefinable greenish-gray color. Later still, after we had been evacuated from The Hague due to the "winter of starvation" in 1944, my father, who had remained behind, was hit by shell splinters on Bezuidenhout Street, during an air raid. He died nine days later, of tetanus. It is a horrible way to go; many years afterward his sister described his dead feet to me, twisted and cramped. In the province of Gelderland I saw a dead pilot, with his intestines hanging out, suspended from the trees by his parachute canopy. And eventually I watched the Germans pull out, ahead of the advancing Canadians and British. Five years earlier, I had seen the Germans arrive; a powerful army, banners and music, serried ranks whose boots made that lisping sound, iron on cobbles, frightful. They bore no resemblance to this when they left. They had already been defeated, you could see that.

Everyone who was alive then will have their own memories of the Liberation. For me that time is associated with the smell of motor cars, leather, and gasoline, with the color of those other uniforms. But most of all with the smell of gasoline that lingered around the jeeps and tanks. We called the men in those jeeps the Liberators, the Canadians, and there was one who always let me sit on his powerful motorcycle—on top of the gas tank. Now, here in Canberra, there is that same smell. It comes from the objects, from the color of the uniforms, the Sam Brownes, the water bottles. Even though there is nothing to smell, I can still smell it, I can even smell what you cannot smell, the sound of the Lancasters flying high above the clouds on their way to bomb Germany. I can smell my own fear, and a bygone time, I can *smell* that I will never be rid of it, and I do not know which thought should go with this smell.

*   *   *

IT STARTS OUTSIDE, in the bright, open air of Canberra. This city is supposed to be the capital of the new Australia, but it is so widely scattered that it hardly qualifies as a city. The new parliament is a modern and imposing green, in contrast to the grave, older shape of the memorial, a mausoleum. Every year on ANZAC Day, Gallipoli Day,* the big march past of the veterans is held here, those who survived commemorating both themselves and the others who did not return. What am I supposed to think of war, of that war? The language of the dioramas is clear enough, it shows abominations, but outside, in front of the memorial, are the old, decommissioned machines of war, black-painted steel glinting in the sunlight. They have become works of art, something they were never intended to be; through their shape they express the aesthetic of death and violence. The tanks are dinosaurs, emulating an extinct animal kingdom. They cannot fade away, their steel is just as hard as it was then. Children run their hands over it. I do too; I cannot resist it. The monstrous cannon that bombarded Amiens during the First World War; Centurion Tank No. 169080, which ran over a mine in Phoc Tuy, Vietnam; the German 210mm howitzer, captured by the 45th Battalion on August 8, 1918 (Germany's Bleak Day).

The parliament building is a long way away, on another hill. The two buildings balance each other out. Each of them expresses something about what this country is. But what is it? When it decided to take part in the First World War Australia was less than 150 years old. It knew that the destruction of the British fleet would endanger its own supply lines, but that does

* ANZAC = Australian New Zealand Army Corps.

not explain the wild enthusiasm with which more than 330,000 men went off to fight in a faraway war, nearly 7 percent of the population, and all by ship! Australia suffered the highest relative number of casualties too: 64.8 percent of the troops that were killed or wounded in the field. From Britain itself that percentage was 49.7. In the Second World War the reason for taking part was more obvious. This time the enemy really was uncomfortably near. With the Japanese in New Guinea it became all too clear what Australia was, and indeed still is: an empty part of the world, chiefly white, at the foot of an enormous and over-populated Asia. When I go in through the huge gateway I read the words: They Gave Their Lives. Nothing more need be said. I see the Eternal Flame, the vulgar coins in the water, but while those few words are still resonating, all of a sudden, with the eye of memory, I also see again the photograph I saw just after the war, and which had such a devastating effect on the boy I was then: the Australian pilot sits on a tree trunk in shorts, blind-folded. Next to him stands a Japanese soldier, two hands on the hilt of his sword which is raised high in the air, catching the sunlight. The Japanese soldier is wearing boots, black jodhpurs, a white shirt. A fraction of a second later that sword will swish down, taking the head of the seated man clean off. I still feel the revulsion I felt then. I walk past the names of the dead; his name, which I never knew, must be among them.

BULLECOURT. IT IS August 11, 1917. Two days after the British go into battle at Arras, the men of the Australian Fourth Brigade attack what remains of the Hindenburg line, near the village of Bullecourt. The tanks that were supposed to break through the barricades of barbed wire did not arrive. The soldiers had lain the entire night in the freezing snow. They were only pulled back the following morning, during a bitter snowstorm. In the evening a fresh attack. This time the tanks are there, but only one gets as far as the barbed wire. You can see what followed on the diorama. The Sixteenth Battalion—men from Western Australia—led by the renowned Major Percy Black, fight their way into the first German trenches. But the battalions of the Twelfth Brigade, who were supposed to come to their aid, are still waiting for their tanks. Because of this the attackers' left flank remains open and vulnerable. Eventually one solitary tank turns up, fires on the waiting Australians by mistake, gets entangled in the German barricades. The brigade now has to advance without any protection whatsoever, and suffers heavy casualties.

War seems to consist for the most part of misunderstandings, but of the type that never come right again. Without artillery support the men nevertheless capture the double row of trenches that form the Hindenburg line. But because the artillery thinks that British tanks are paving the way for the Australians, they refrain from fire and this gives the Germans the opportunity to get a cordon of artillery and machine guns in place behind the Australians, cutting them off from supplies and reinforcements. What follows is six long hours of desperate man-to-man combat, until the Australians run out of ammunition and are forced to retreat through the barricades, under fire. The division's losses are heavy: 857 dead, including Major Black; 1,275 taken prisoner; more than a thousand wounded. The chilling thing about the frozen theater in front of me is the silence. No swearing, no last scream, no sound of feet in the frozen snow, no explosions, no sound of the bayonets piercing dust and flesh, not even the quiet of the winter's night, which, in among all those other sounds, must surely have had a different sound.

ON MY TOUR, I almost trip over a man sitting in the mud. He is so dreadfully realistic that I recoil. He is coated in mire, his shoes, his leggings. He has covered his eyes with his hands, he no longer wants to see the world. The helmet, so straight on his head, has suddenly become a strange thing, an obscure sort of crown. A child standing next to me reaches out her hand toward him, and yes, you do want to touch him, console him. But you remain standing where you are. Not because it is a statue, but because it is no longer possible to console him. His *now* is a *then*. But it is the same as with the watch belonging to the sergeant from Queensland, something that expresses duration and standstill simultaneously, something done with while at the same time still continuing. The man who charges to the attack, screaming, running toward his death, getting shot, thinking a last, forever private thought; all that can never be undone, even if it is eventually forgotten by everyone. Memorial, place of remembrance. The longer this place exists, the more abstract the wars it commemorates will become, stranger, separated from the significance they had for contemporaries. What will be left to see then? A man in the mud, whose fate is added to the deaths of the others, so that they too are sitting in the mud with their hands covering their eyes, because they no longer want to see the world.

There are lots of children at the memorial. I notice how the girls have a different way of looking from the boys. It is not just that they are more inclined to look at the nurses, the women soldiers, the hairstyles of the time (which have now been revived as today's hairdos). No, they look in a different way too at the congealed fighting, the weaponry, planes, bullets, and knives. I cannot define that look, but it has something to do with an ancient reserve. It is not the adventure, the gleam of diving Spitfires in a doomed sky, the pathetic gesticulation of the sinking ship, the red flames licking around the torched village, but the thinking that lies behind it all, and that has to do with destruction. They observe in a different way, walk more quietly. Neither do they laugh when, on a roll of film from '14 to '18, the soldiers walk in such a strange, shaky, speeded-up way, and the tanks move around in crazily brisk fashion, like a computer game. It is as if the girls have a different rhythm of time, and are therefore able to slow down those speeded-up movements—due simply to a lack of technique—so that all of a sudden there are live men struggling through the mud, men who are long dead now, but who still walk abroad, much slower, even, than their eye can see.

All this makes you a voyeur, someone who sees something but cannot himself be seen. You recognize those others over there, walking along so quickly, but they do not recognize you. You know something they do not know, how things turn out, their fate. You even permit yourself some doubts about the point of their death, a posthumous intrusion that is inadmissible. So the past becomes inaccessible at the very place where this same past is revealed—the paradox of a place of commemoration.

KIENHOLZ, I HAVE already mentioned the name. His interiors also enable you to look without anyone seeing you. The reflective prism of art: whereas Kienholz obtains his material from observed reality, I see reality through the prism of just such a replication. The Battle of Menen, September 1917. "A Brigade Headquarters," a photograph. It appears to be underground, and as with a Kienholz the objects acquire a magical, autonomous meaning. Three burning candles. Helmets hanging from the rough-beamed ceiling. A bottle of soda water. Wet clothes. A box of matches. They lie on the table diagonally, so imbued with sudden meaning that it seems they would fain be a thousand boxes of matches at once. This effect is produced by the enclosed nature of the space. Three men, one of them is trying to get a connection, earpiece to his ear. A topographic map. A mug. A water bottle. A tin of tobacco. Not one of those men looks up to see us; we are the forbidden creatures from beyond their deaths, unborn nothingness, posthumous museum visitors. Nonexistence, the mutual lure of the photograph: while we exist, they do not, and while they exist, we do not. But it is an imperfect reciprocity: they will never look at a photograph of us. They can do without us, we are only here for the memory. They were busy with other things, the Battle of Menen, for instance.

AT THE END of my tour I come across George. George is a Lancaster. I have never set eyes on one before, but its sound is one I will remember to the end of my days. "Will" is the wrong word, though, for George will never fly again. It used to fly overhead, far too high to see, together with its brothers in arms, en route to Germany. I have often attempted to describe that sound, I do not think it is possible. A freak flight of monotone metal bumblebees, the continuous, long-drawn-out drone of a hundred basses. This goes some way, but not near enough, for nothing can convey the threat and promise contained within that sound. There go *"de Engelsen,"* on their way to bomb Germany. Now perhaps the war will soon be over. They were off to punish the Germans, to flatten German cities. You could not see them, only hear them. First from far off, then overhead, a mysterious vibrating that seemed to affect everything, then further and further away, impervious to the barking of the ack-ack guns. I must have heard George too, for it flew more than ninety missions above occupied Europe. The Royal Australian Air Force took delivery of it in 1942. It was hit thirty times, yellow bombs are painted on its side, pointing downward, one for each mission. By 1944 it had had its day, and was allowed to return to Australia. G for George: in the suddenly small hall it is stupendously big, an inexplicable dead bird, which still towers over you threateningly, a heavy shadow. I try to imagine it staying here forever, and how it will gradually become stranger and stranger, until there is nobody left any more who believes it ever flew.

EMERGING INTO the brilliant sunshine I almost collide with the sculpture of a man with a donkey. It is a small donkey, its head bowed as it descends the hill. On its back it carries a wounded man, long legs almost touching the ground. The other man walks beside the donkey, has it on a rope but does not need to lead it, the donkey can find the way by itself. The man's name is Simpson, but they called him "the man with the donkey." For three whole weeks he collected the wounded from the front line at Gallipoli, and brought them through the crossfire on his donkey, to the beach and the ships. At the end of the third week he was hit by a sniper, during the Turkish offensive of May 19. Now he is made of bronze, Simpson, and he still goes down his endless hill. The donkey's nose shines because everyone wants to touch it, well, yes, stroke it. Perhaps they would really like to touch the man too, albeit briefly, just give him a nudge, a sort of "Hello there, Simpson"—but that is not possible.

DECEMBER 1989

The Gardener and Death

P.N. van Eyck
Translated from the Dutch by James Brockway

This morning, pale, aghast, my gardener ran
Into my house: Master, I must be gone!

I was working, pruning roses, unaware,
And there stood Death and fixed me with his stare.

Afraid, I dashed away as fast as could be,
Yet saw him raise his hand and threaten me.

My lord, your horse, your spurs, let me be gone.
Before nightfall I'll be in Ispahan!

Long had he fled, and as the day grew dark,
Death I encountered in the cedar park.

Why, I demand (for he waits and no word will he say)
Did you threaten my gardener earlier today?

Smiling, he makes reply: My gesture meant
No threat to him; it was astonishment

To find him working here this morn, the man
Whom I must seize tonight in Ispahan.

P.N. van Eyck (1887–1954), Dutch poet. The poem is an adaptation
of a Persian legend and is itself a Dutch classic.

An Evening in Isfahan

TRUMAN CAPOTE would never fly on a Friday, and it tends to scare me too. And getting older doesn't make it easier. You read a poem (twenty, twenty-five years ago), and from that day on Isfahan represents unavoidable fate, the spot where death will catch up with you. For years I have wanted to go there; I always assumed I would never return. And it is not just me it has this effect on. Walking around Amsterdam's Schiphol airport on the morning of my departure, I bump into Donner, the chess master. He is traveling to Munich for an international competition. I tell him I am going to Isfahan. He looks concerned. "I'd be careful if I were you!" But by then it is too late. I have already procured my fate, and a few hours later I am flying over the Balkans in a German aircraft, full to the last seat with businessmen. I am on my way to a poem, they to a boom country. It is an accurate foretaste of what is to come. Teheran has become gold-rush city, the only difference being that the gold diggers tote attaché cases instead of shovels. All the hotels are full; in every newspaper there are photographs of German, Japanese, and Italian delegations hovering around the Shah, like courtiers around the Sun King. A stewardess hands outs the *Kayhan,* a Persian newspaper in English. His Imperial Majesty the Shahanshah urges a steel mill for Khorassan; Iran and India reach full understanding; Suryanaran Veena plays Carnatic

music in the City Theater at 8 PM; and, fresh proof of how dense
I can be when it comes to ordinary facts: I suddenly realize that I
am flying toward the East for the first time, and *because* I realize it,
three things occur simultaneously, one factual (it is rapidly getting
dark), two sentimental: I have a physical sensation of flying over
something very ancient, over something that stretches, empty
and endless. Both are true, but to have a physical sensation is
strange; for while I am musing on the peacock throne, Xenophon,
Herodotus, and Zarathustra, the means of transport in which I am
sitting is trundling toward a place that could just as well be to the
west or north. Anyhow, it takes five hours, and it is after midnight
by the time I walk across a tarmac reeking of gas, past a couple of
monstrous military planes, toward chaos.

Arriving anywhere for the first time always has something of
a psychological test about it. First test: all the hotels are full, what
do you do now? Nothing, wait and badger. Second test: bawling
men carry your luggage outside, then want money. Money that
only has Arabic characters on it. And how much is how much?
Next, other, similar men arrive, who load your luggage on to a car
roof, but take you off to wait in a queue. Pushing and protesting in
the Eastern night air, a long queue, a long wait, but the ticket you
eventually purchase entitles you to a taxi. So no swindle. A clever
system in fact, if you did but know.

The streets are wide, empty. I see shadowy high buildings.
The hotel is a set for a spy film, *anno* 1942. Humphrey Bogart is
manning the reception desk, but I keep the microfilms under my
toupee for the time being. A cracked celluloid sheen hangs over
everything, panels of old marble cover the pillars, rubber plants
are sunk in morbid reverie, and guess what: Persian carpets!

The walls of my room are finished in old-newspaper yellow.
Your secret agent turns back the bedclothes and spies a long,

winding hair; there is water from the bathroom on the floor, and when I move the only chair the plastic shutters make an irritating, rattling sound. I am home. I sit down on that chair, on which an entire population has sat, and unfold the map of Teheran. As soon as I arrive anywhere a kind of gluttony takes hold of me—I have to know how it all fits together, I have to fathom out the "system" of the city, have to walk, sniff, observe, sit in buses and trams, make the city my own.

In the limbo of the hotel a clock chimes. I start to unpack my case and discover that I have forgotten my sponge bag. When I was in the taxi, I noticed a drugstore around the corner that was still open. I head for it. It is pleasant out. The drugstore is called Takhte Jamshid, a white neon strip in a wall of darkness. It has everything I need, and it all comes from abroad, right down to the nail scissors. The problems of the Third World made simple for children. I pay with a greenish banknote that has a sort of heart with a dot on it, but this is greeted with guffaws of laughter. What a crazy foreign fellow! I let them select the right one themselves, conscious of the fact that had I been German, I would have learned the numerals from one to ten at least, off by heart. Resolving to do just that, I hand my imported bits and pieces in at reception, and go back outside.

A strange sensation, as if it would be but a minute's work, despite the extremely solid impression it makes, to lift the city off this wild, empty old plain, the way a jungle reclaims a deserted encampment. Later on I learn that this "plain" is anything but. The "plateau" the experts refer to is high and rugged. Teheran climbs from 1,200 to 1,700 meters; there are deserts, steppes, and malevolently high, snow-capped mountains in Persia; various climates, various peoples. "If," writes Jean Hureau, "the Ararat mountain, where the Russian, Turkish and Persian borders converge, lay in

Paris, then the Persian–Pakistan border would lie beyond Athens, the border with Afghanistan beyond Budapest. Teheran would lie in Venice and Shiraz in Naples." It is an empire within which various peoples are united, just like it was in the ages of Cyrus, Darius, and Xerxes. The name *Iran* comes from the Aryans, or Arians, an Indo-European people who, from about 4000 BC, migrated from the northwest, across the River Oxus into the country. They spoke one language, kept horses, rode in chariots, and moved gradually westward. The heart of their domain was the Fars region. Hence the name *Persia*.

I do my homework until my eyes fall shut, and am woken next morning by the warmth, and by a constant humming sound. I part the blinds slightly to see an enormous dove-gray crow and a panther-like wildcat, and behind them a massive flow of traffic, thick as treacle and smoking from every orifice. Ten minutes later I get my first Persian lesson: the taxi dance. It takes a while to get the hang of it, and it never really gets easy. You have to position yourself on the roadway. As soon as a small, orange taxi approaches you throw yourself at it and yell your destination through the open window—in Persian learned by heart beforehand. This can never be your ultimate destination, however, as taxis make their way across the city exclusively in straight lines. So if you wish to go eastward, and then southward, you need to carry out the whole operation twice. The driver will have slowed down imperceptibly, but they only stop definitively if they decide to take your fare. The criteria for whether they do or not remains shrouded in mystery. Usually they shoot off again. Your first priority at this stage is to save your life, for all Persian taxi drivers carry within them a deep desire to revenge themselves for those one million years of car-lessness. Red lights, pedestrians, human lives, none of it worth a row of beans—away with it! They hammer along the streets like the wrath of God. Once you do manage to get a taxi, you will find yourself sharing it with up to five people, and from inside you will be able to observe others outside, desperately performing the taxi dance. But they always get you there, and it costs next to nothing.

I alight at the bazaar. Shut off from the rest of the world, it is a covered cosmos of markets, bakers, coppersmiths, tea houses, money changers, butchers, herbalists. Because I am always happiest in these sorts of places I have never asked myself why. We do seem to spend less time thinking about happiness than about unhappiness. Perhaps it is because of an awareness that what for us is a jumble and a labyrinth, actually contains within it a simple and straightforward order, but one which we can never be party to. The semblance of a riddle always pleases me more than the fact of a solution, and so I sit there most contentedly, on the steps next to the coppersmith, hearing the metallic ringing, seeing how the arabesques are hammered into the copper, watching people actually *making* things, the manufacturer not yet alienated from his product—this is a crucial aspect too of course, everybody doing what he *is*, the way a writer writes and a farmer sows. So that the world is managed by its people, instead of its people by the world. The smith is the smith, the herbalist the herbalist, the gardener is the gardener, and death is death.

Is this true? It is not entirely true, but true it is, nevertheless. Soon it will not be true any longer. There will come a time when all this copperware will be made by machine, and the person presently making the copperware will make the machine. When this happens both he and the object he makes will have become something different, and the place where I watched him at work, and saw how this making something comes about, will be an empty space. Not yet, though. I stroll through the wafting smells, touching things, looking at people; I eat a bowl of *dugh*, a type of yogurt, drink fresh carrot juice, and all at once find myself in the courtyard of a mosque. The shock of light, and the shock of silence. In the center is a square-shaped water fountain containing a greenish liquid and a few jets of water. I sit on the edge. To the left of me a man is washing his hands, again and again. A boy comes and stands next to me, takes off his ring, bends forward, and immerses his entire face in the water. The only slight sound is made by the water. After their ablutions, they cross the wide courtyard to a large alcove lit by the sun, and join the men already there, each one individually saying his prayers. I have a feeling I should not be watching so unashamedly, but that is because they are praying so unashamedly. Like the saints whose lives I used to read about, they are lost to the world. One of them sits, turns his arms outwards, raises up his hands, bows forward, stands up again, then bows down to the ground, eyes shut, lips moving. At the same time, others are performing different movements, lifting up their hands, staring at the heavens, bowing and swaying; some are wearing kaftans, their shoes and slippers lined up in a long row in front of the alcove. Still more are arriving, different head-dresses, facial features, tribes; broad Mongolian bone structure, nomads, Arabian scholars with Borges faces. Nothing is more dismal than progress, thinks the rational progressive and senti-mental regressive that I am, who feels a shiver of despondency whenever he sees a group of black-garbed Christian dogs in his own fatherland coming out of church with similar piety. Perplexed by such inner contradictions I wander away from this courtyard of silence, exiling myself from the vice of their profundity.

The following day I am off to Persia proper. That day the Shah shuffles the cards of his cabinet once again; the streets are hung with placards proclaiming "Welcome Indira"; a form of urban land reform is announced, including extremely severe penalties for speculators in building land. Christina Gascoigne, the English photographer with whom I am to make the journey, has arrived too. She speaks Persian, was born in Iraq, and with her tall, bird-like figure and Virginia Woolf profile she throws the Persians into confusion.

THE SUN IS SHINING, and we are sitting in the back of a big American car, having been unable to arrange a *hire-drive*. The right-angled network of streets that is Teheran disappears, and we reach the suburbs, where the plain is already visible, heralded by dust and sand. Leaving behind the anarchy of the traffic, we pass the last usurious shops of the money changers, their windows full of gold coins and banknotes, pass Papadopoulos's tailor, *tailleur grec*, and the last few tea houses, where large gatherings of men sit slurping their water pipes. And then it is done with.

Emptiness, endlessness, aridity, hundreds of kilometers of it en route to Isfahan, faint mountains in the distance, the empty halls of the world between Europe and Asia. No gas stations, no roadside restaurants, no temptation, bare and stifling, with the golden dome of the mosque at Qum, the holy city of pilgrimage, appearing like a mirage in the middle of the day. Pilgrims from all over Persia come here, a multitude who can quickly turn fanatical and who do not take kindly to strangers. To enter the mosque is forbidden, you can feel the tension in the air if you get too near. Extraordinary, this power of attraction exerted by the forbidden. I can feel myself being repeatedly drawn to that gateway through which I am not allowed to go. I see gold braid, cloaks, and turbans, but when I dally too long they point to the multilingual signs forbidding entry in no uncertain terms. We head for the hotel opposite the mosque, a hotel for pilgrims. No European dress, all the notices in Arabic, the pretensions of English to being a global language evaporate like eau de Cologne. I am reduced to a pointer and an unintelligible stutterer, yet even so a little while later warm nan arrives at our table, with pungent cheese, raw onion, and herbs. There is also a bowl of the whitest, shiniest rice I have ever seen. We wrap some of the cheese, rice and onions in the nan. Beer and wine are not served, but there is tea and *dughabali*, yogurt with ice and mineral water from the mountains. The rice is dressed with *mast*, a thicker type of yogurt, and we sprinkle it with *sumac*, a spice obtained from minced tree root. And to add to it all, at twelve o'clock the rambling but penetrating, interminable call of the muezzin splits the heavens, so loudly that the glasses on the table shake, a voice that reaches all over town, and seeps into every part of my body. And it goes on and on, I am trapped within that sound and feel far removed from everything I know. Outside, the bluish-gray and brown kaftans billow past, white turbans, closely shaven heads swathed in black headbands; a different, older time. Our bill is totted up on an abacus; we cross the main square once more, the defiant gold of the minaret pointing upward like a clenched fist. Pilgrims have been coming here for more than a thousand years, we are a mere sigh that fades away, unseen.

The surrounding landscape contains every color except the cheerful ones. Sharp, jagged mountains have been placed on top of it, around each bend the punishment begins anew, the empty waiting rooms of history. Sometimes there are pathetic car wrecks along the route, in the distance a herd's black shadow. A sun-scorched man sits motionless by the side of the road, hand outstretched. The driver stops and gives him something. I wander a short distance into scrub and break off the stem of a dry plant: the sap inside smells of the earth, arid and old, immensely old.

The key word is old. You approach Persia with blind Western arrogance and find yourself confronted by thousands of years of history without any point of reference. The last thing you ever learned was Xerxes, but what about all those centuries that came afterward? It is rather like going to France without knowing about the French Revolution, with the vaguest possible notion of Napoleon, and with no conception whatsoever of Charlemagne, the spread of Christendom, and the difference between Catholicism and Protestantism. No easy matter! Cyrus conquered the Medes and founded the Achaemenid dynasty. That was in 550 BC. Alexander defeated the Persians at both Issus and Arbela. A new dynasty, the Seleucids, followed. Then another, the Parthians, nomads, who kept the Romans at bay. And yet another, the Sassanids, more powerful than Rome and Byzantium. They left behind their larger-than-life-size royal graves in the gold-colored rocks of Naqshi-i-Rustam. Then it is the turn of Islam. Caliph Omar conquers the country in 642, and indeed the Persians remain Islamic to this day, although they are extremely conscious of having a history far more ancient than Islam, and of having once been defeated by the Arabs. The schismatic form of Islam, which the Persians practice, called Shiism, has its own successors to Mohammed, and is considered heretical by other Muslims. Whatever the case, Mohammed and his doctrine have determined Persian history since the seventh century. The Seljuks, from the steppes of Central Asia, whose Mongoloid features you still see all around you, rule until 1187. Then, like the crack of a whip, Genghis Khan arrives, followed one century later by the all-consuming fire of Tamerlane. But the Timurid dynasty (1380–1499), which he founded, built upon the blackened ruins left by their forefather. They left behind buildings of a terrifying simplicity. This sounds exaggerated, but after a morning spent beneath the brick vaulting of the Friday mosque in Isfahan, you know better. It is an architecture that seems to have been fashioned by nature, of a purity which it is impossible to exaggerate. Only after this does Isfahan's golden age arrive, but all the splendor, all the dazzling constructions and faiences cannot for one second compete with the shock I received that morning in the Friday mosque. The Timurids depart, the Safavids arrive. This dynasty is as important as the Bourbons are for France, the Hapsburgs for Spain. Tell a Persian you do not know who Shah Abbas is and you evoke a deep and intense commiseration. This Sun King turned Isfahan into the most splendid jewel of his age. Popes and emperors sent their ambassadors to gaze at this wonder of the world, and it was then that the name Isfahan acquired its mysterious allure, which is the reason why, hundreds of years later, I still feel a strange sense of excitement as I approach the city through the searing landscape.

Actually, this landscape provides the perfect introduction. There is no way flying in could give you the same physical appreciation of the contrast between Persia proper and the Persian coast. The dream dreamed by a man who lives in the desert is a dream of oases, shelter, flowers, colors, pleasure, burbling brooks. And it is true—after the stone you understand the rose, after the rose you can tolerate the stone. You shut out the parched enormity of the outside world, and within, on tiles, minarets, and carpets, enjoy the flowers and the colors, the grace that failed outside.

How do you describe the dome of a mosque? One aspect of Arabic art is its nonhumanity, that images of human beings are excluded. There is no identification with drama, feeling, history. You walk around in a permanent state of bliss, each form more sophisticated, more sensual, more perfect than the one before, and you keep on looking until, in my case, a dazzled sort of blindness takes hold, and all the labyrinthine geometric figures and their tints become a blur of color, as if the kaleidoscope has melted from all that looking.

We are staying in the Shah Abbas hotel, which is a legend in itself. An implausibly large antique and bric-a-brac shop, set in a frozen meringue, which itself encloses a deathly quiet rose garden. Silent valets, belonging to a genus that died out long ago in the rest of the world, nest in the niches of the corridors and flap hither and thither with unhurried wing beats. It has all the allure of an old film, but not to live in. After a few days you feel as though you yourself are well on the way to becoming an extinct species; first it is 1940, then 1920, 1880, and only the arrival of the highly contemporary hotel bill brings us down to earth with a bang.

But the problem remains: how do you describe a dome, a mosque, and a city full of domes and mosques? I feel I am constantly on the outside of all this splendor, admiring it but unable to penetrate it. To put it at its most banal: there is nothing there—a craving for decoration and geometry elevated to a passion, hashish-dreams spiraling up into the pure, bluish-white air. Even the domes, made of stone after all, of earth, of *thing*, seem transparent; multicolored soap bubbles of enormous proportions, secured to the earth by mysterious sorcery. I cannot fathom it. Each morning, from the window of my room, I see the dome of the Madraseh-ye Madar-e Shah, the theological college, erected in 1706. I have discovered a secret route across the roof of the hotel, so I can get up close, where it becomes more amenable. The geometric madness of the minaret sobers up to become glazed tiles arranged in patterns, the vertigo of perpendicular, white festoons (I now know that festoons can be straight) is unmasked as an interminable calligraphic quote from the Koran. The dome itself is a shining silk carpet that contravenes all the laws of physics, ballooning out in gold, violet, and turquoise. And each time the eye grows tired, it beats a hurried retreat to a human form; a mullah in a kaftan sitting reading a book by a fountain, a couple of students strolling arm in arm past the rose borders, talking about something I can have no notion of. The archway they walk under resembles a man-made Fingal's Cave, each stalactite a jewel set among other jewels. It all radiates a barbarous beauty, and by the end I notice that after all the later, maddening mihrabs, minarets, and *eivans*, I must return again and again to the Friday mosque, the oldest, simplest, and, strange to say, the "holiest"—just as in early Gothic or Romanesque churches you get the feeling that the old man over in the corner could well be God, driven out of his later, loftier space stations by an excess of splendor.

Two boys are praying in the middle of the empty, open square. The orderly heavens float above the square and in those heavens the disorderly clouds, the way everything now either does or does not form part of this compulsive order. Cawing malignantly, crows swoop from *eivan* to *eivan*, chasing away the pigeons. Each time you look back, after momentarily focusing elsewhere, you see how the light crashes down onto the great square—light and heavens have simply been annexed by this architecture, becoming lamp and ceiling.

Walking away from the courtyard I come to a forest of stone pillars, beneath a canopied heaven of stone. Two women, almost completely hidden in black *chorbas*, flap past me and disappear behind a door, from where soft, lamenting singing issues. I peer through the keyhole and see an old man in a white turban, rocking back and forth. Apart from this it is very quiet. The occasional minor explosion of a pigeon taking wing beneath the vaulting, which extends wherever you look. Only when you peer "outside" do you see once again the lofty openwork of that blue façade, a cave filled with treasure, and when you head back toward it you are oppressed anew by the fantastic order of the decoration, where caprice is only tolerated if repeated until becoming wholly compulsive. I examine it while running my hand over the alabaster of a pillar. The tiny grooves, formed a thousand years ago, feel sensual to my touch. Something I have never experienced with stone before. There is light everywhere, flooding, pooling, piercing, threading; the very stones have been embroidered with it, pigeons fly in and out of it.

I take another way out of the mosque and find myself in the middle of a popular quarter, among mud dwellings. A guide (recognizable anywhere) extricates himself from the crowd milling around a textile stall. I do not want a guide, I want to be alone, but he perseveres, keeping up a steady patter, walking ahead of me with his almost perky goose-step, and eventually I give in. We visit a baker, who is flattening the large pancake-like rounds of dough against the outside of his piping-hot oven with a cushion, we go to see dilapidated houses whose murals have been clumsily restored, sit in a small park where students are stretched out studying, or pacing back and forth, mumbling audibly. Bravely he flits ahead of me through the Jewish quarter ("they no good, they is not like us"), into an underground factory half lit by oil lamps, where a resigned camel turns a centuries-old treadmill, causing a complicated wooden cogwheel to press linseed oil. After each thing we see, he says contentedly: "This has been very good, very, very, good," and when we part he congratulates me: "I hope you has learnt. Like someone who has thirsty drink one two three, so you have gained from the knowledge of the world."

So I have, and I do the taxi dance once more—they are light blue around here. However, we are immediately cleared from the road by majestic police outriders on motorcycles, who are literally sweeping the streets clean. "Indira," the taxi driver yells excitedly, and sure enough, a long green limousine, into which at least five of his taxis would fit, floats past. The handsome, hawk-like profile of Mrs. Gandhi barely emerges above door height. A small hand waving languidly, and she is gone. An hour later when I arrive at the hotel, her car is parked on the forecourt. The red carnations lying in the back are already turning dark.

And so our days in Isfahan slip by. Occasionally I remember that Someone is supposed to be coming for me, but it will presumably be in a place that rhymes with something else, for I feel far removed from everything, and reasonably immortal. The *Kayhan* is my sole link with current events. The Shah receives one delegation after another, gives advice, and admonishes: "Monarch warns against lagging in productivity," "The Shahanshah on Saturday clarified major obstacles to progress in Iran."

Indeed, there seems to be nothing that he does *not* involve himself with. "Schools must be built in close proximity to those who need them. And if this is costly, well, it cannot be helped." "Acquisition and sale of land for speculative purposes can never be truly productive." "If there is a shortage of meat, it is the government's fault." "Our farmers have to put up with a lower standard of living than the rest of the population, as if they are still being colonised, purely to keep prices low for the consumer." "Why does the press express surprise at the increase in the price of accumulators, without informing their readers about the reason? Why do they not express surprise that a ton of cement costs 1,800 rials here, and 6,000 rials abroad?"

Many observers, however, both within Persia and without, question the relevance of these and similar comments, although of course there is no denying that the country is being dragged steadily and with ever increasing speed out of the darkness of feudalism.

I HAVE BEEN saturated with Isfahan, and feel as if I have almost become an arabesque myself. I awake during the night, hear the crows cawing, and stick my head out of the window into the overwhelming rose scent of the garden. The moon is shining on the dome of the mosque, the crows are perched, suddenly silent, on the white garden chairs. As soon as the light comes creeping, from all around you hear the sound of the muezzins, carried on the wind the way it was a hundred, five hundred, even a thousand years ago. I have eaten caviar from the Caspian Sea, strange fish from the Persian Gulf, head of lamb complete with tongue, brains and one eye. I have drunk wine from Shiraz that fosters a heavy sort of dreaming that must have been the cause of Omar Khayyám's melancholia. Enough is enough. I climb the steep tribune of the Ali Qapu, one last time. The big square, the *maidan*, lies at my feet, and where I stand the mighty emperor, Shah Abbas, once stood, lay, or sat, while watching the polo matches and races far below him. On such occasions the sides of the big terrace would be closed off, the silk curtains billowing in the wind. Ambassadors from Europe and the Far East, traveling scholars, Jesuits, Indian princes, all were drawn to this steep, wooden terrace, this hub of empire. The same mast-high wooden pillars still support the roof, and behind the terrace a rabbit warren of stairs and small rooms is situated. Through openings in the wall the blazing vision of a mosque's dome is sometimes visible. Birds with exotic plumage cling to the ceilings; rosettes, stylized palm leaves, the giddying dazzle of inlaid glass—there is too much of it, too much. In the park behind stands the palace, its twenty pillars reflected into forty by the dark green, deathly quiet water. Here, at last, I see walls painted with representations of the human form. People! It comes as a relief after all the geometry: faces, hands clasping pomegranates, fingers banging a tambourine, feet that are dancing, almond-shaped, olive-black eyes set like jewels, upturned moustaches, breasts, "the moons of paradise": sycophants, dancers, informants, jesters, heroes; a Persian court—and wave upon wave of warriors, rearing horses, a knight cleft in twain, his eyes those of that lamb's head on my plate yesterday: a Persian battle. Oh, to be able to eat from those dishes, but you cannot eat painted food; it has perished and been preserved, like those who ate it, like the jingling of the bells on the ankles of the dancers, beneath their brocade skirts, like the fingers on the pipes of Pan, the grapes between the raspberry-red lips, the falcons on the princes' gauntlets. Away from here and into the desert, away from these verdant, distant landscapes of painted time.

THE JOURNEY continues to Yazd, the town where the Zoroastrians still live: fire worshippers, guardians of the oldest religion, venerators of Ahura Mazda, who is portrayed with stiff outstretched wings, above the head of King Darius, on the walls of Persepolis. He predates Alexander, predates Christ, predates Mohammed, who drove him from Persia but not from Yazd. The road is endless, no longer asphalted, even a traffic sign is an event. The desert appears to be made of water, I am positive the raised parts of the terrain are floating upon it. There is no possibility of food or drink en route. Sometimes, a four-wheeled monster, visible more than half an hour away as a dust storm, thunders by, headlights glaring in the daylight. We arrive in Yazd dehydrated and deadbeat. At the hotel we can chose between a SINGEL, a DABAL or a THREE bed; CONeiYAK is available per BOTER or in ONe pice, and should you not want cognac, there is always CANADArY, Beer Tobork, DRINKING COLD, COCACO or HOT CHOaCOLTE. Evening arrives, bringing that sweet white light that is so delicious in the subtropics. It is lukewarm with a whisper of coolness; carbide lamps hiss, fires flicker, and all at once I know why I always feel such a sense of well-being in towns like this. All those highfalutin ideas about ancient crafts and customs and the survival of traditional family ties suddenly seem flimsy rationalizations: it is all about being cozy and inviting. You wander through it in the dusk, among the shouts and whispers, the figures shrouded in veils, a town somewhere on the unending plain between East and West. Without the aggressive modernity of Teheran, without the stupefying brilliance of Isfahan, just an Eastern town—some place, no place—with a muddled square and a large mosque with niches in the outside wall, where groups of men slouch, chat, cook, and pray, or lie asleep, dead to the world. Cooking scents, faces illuminated by arm-sized wax candles, five boys leaning against a mud wall, their giggling angel-faces, sometimes the gray senseless glare of a television in a darkened room, shops full of large slabs of sugar and candy, bags of dried fruit to take with you, should fate decide to send you away from this oasis, out into the dry wastes where your house is one, two, three days' journey away.

WHAT DOES A FIRE worshipper look like? Ordinary, with a white coat and a white cap. A guide has taken us to the temple. The contrast with the Muslim districts is immediately apparent: here the women are not veiled, and they wear light, brightly colored dresses. The temple is a small, low building in a damp, almost Dutch garden. The priest, or whatever he is, looks like a surgeon who performs every operation with a smile. He takes us to see an enormous copper cauldron behind bars, inside which a fire is burning.

This has been burning for forty-five years, he says, not without pride. There are no flames escaping; it has a deep, incredibly intense glow, which, if you gaze into it for long enough, begins to stare back. It smells of incense.

On the wall "Sorab Pinthewalla, 1951, Bombay," has painted

an itinerant Zoroastrian preacher. It is very quiet. A woman sits praying, a fiery block is sinking very slowly into the white ash, the priest lights a fresh stick of incense, the sexton proffers a collection box. I wander back to the painting, and wonder whether the prophet portrayed has really something to do with Nietzsche's Zarathustra. This one is pointing ecstatically heavenward, a yellow sash waving in his wake. Behind him glows a peony-red sunset, and with his left hand he is touching a barren sandhill with his staff. Fiery beams of light surround his wise head. The priest tells us that under the Shah's regime they have freedom of worship, but are not permitted to bury their dead the way they were used to, namely by *not* doing so. Corpses were laid out on the highest rock, or on top of a "Tower of Silence," and left to be devoured by dogs, crows, and vultures. Only when not a single ounce of flesh remained would the skeleton be interned in an *astodan*, a house of bones hacked out in the rocks, facing the sun. All this was done because, otherwise, when the life force left the body, the demon of the corpse would spread his poison everywhere.

And why the fire?

He draws my attention to the large crown high above it. "Because the Fire, it is holy." It drives away evil spirits, and attracts the gods.

Outside Yazd, I climb a Tower of Silence. The sun has just risen, and glances off the snow of the distant mountains. The towers of the dead are high and hollow-eyed, their mud torsos dead and bare themselves. The silence is devastating. I drag myself up the endless stairs like one condemned. Far below me is a graveyard where I can hear men laughing, and that is that. I stand there for a while looking at the landscape, and wonder just how old the tower is. A thousand years? Thousands? Below, in the desert I can see the elegant traces of the *qanats*, ancient underwater canals, some of which are more than forty kilometers long.

This is Persia at its most ancient; with each tread I take down the Calvary-like steps I shrug off another layer of antiquity, arriving down again at precisely the same time as the invention of the motor car, which I promptly climb into and drive off in for days, through a long tunnel of sun, toward Shiraz.

City of wine, roses, and verse, where the great poets Hafiz and Sadi lie buried in regal splendor, and where Persian farmers come to have their photographs taken next to the graves of these poets of centuries ago, and also to recite their poetry out loud to one another. Where else would you still find that? They are blithe days, these final days in Shiraz. The gardens are cool, lush, full of flowers that split open orgiastically, secret lanes, irises like orchids. The wine has a heavy, almost savage taste and I can well understand how it made Hafiz and Khayyám so utterly joyful and so stupefyingly sad, but, as I wrote to an old friend, I have survived Isfahan, and as long as I never return my end will be played out in a place from another poem. And what of it, says Omar Khayyám, for,

> Imagine life is one long party—and then?
> The final day dawns at last—and then?
> Look forward to a full hundred years,
> And another hundred years thrown in—and then?

THERE IS NOT THE slightest chance of approaching the grave of Cyrus circumspectly: there it lies in the middle of the plain, empty, powerful, and ineluctable, with the wind racing through it. To the right, a few rolling brown hills, which in the far distance become low, hazy mountains. And above, the same clouds as always. High, green grass surrounds the grave itself. To the left, behind some high fencing, a group of nomads with donkeys and sheep. Their clothes are brightly colored, their features Mongolian;

the women are not wearing veils. They have the look and gait of liberated people.

The grave is lofty, the individual steps are almost waist-high, only a giant could climb them "normally." But the power that these steps exude is not that of the monarch—his power stemmed from Ahura Mazda—he was merely its earthly vehicle, the mediator between the people and the deity. The grave is silent and looks down at you no matter where you position yourself, the way the eyes in certain paintings follow you around the room. Twice, Alexander the Great stood here in front of the golden Sarcophagus, the first time at the zenith of his campaign, to pay tribute to the already legendary deceased. The second time, six years later, to punish the men who had plundered the tomb.

Some way off from the grave lie ruins. A mysterious wingéd man slowly disappears into the stone from which someone once hewed him. The man behind him is pointing out an invisible "something" to this stranger. The four-wingéd one is wearing an Elamitic cloak. On his head the divine, triple crown of Egypt. The aftermath of the sunset frets at the zinc-colored clouds, and watchmen, different ones this time, tell us we should go. We leave the riddle behind. Who was it? Cyrus himself? A guardian demon? Nobody knows. On another remaining, half-ruined wall, the words "I, Cyrus, the King, an Achaemenid, built this" can still be made out in three languages: ancient Persian, Elamitic, Babylonian (all three perished, evaporated, and no tongue will ever speak them again). A stork perches on the only pillar left standing. As we drive away it is already dark. The nomads have set up their tents. Their fires are burning. Even in the blackness of night the grave still forms a black void.

*   *   *

The lion kills the bull at the foot of the long terraces of Persepolis, and the visitor sees the same death endlessly repeated, an eternal one moment: the position of the zodiac is the place where he stands. Persepolis was the astrological center of the universe, far more of a religious than a secular capital, dedicated to the Almighty Ahura Mazda, in the Zoroastrian religion the incarnation of Goodness. Darius, or Daryarush in Zoroastrian, built Persepolis in 550 BC. The weird thing about our era is that the shadow of Christ is also cast backwards, somewhere it does not belong at all: the period before he even existed and which his followers, by counting backwards, have usurped for him. But how absent he is here! Here on this cool, upland plain you encounter the rarefied clarity of the period before history became condensed into that clotted mass of complications, which eventually gets handed down to us as the "present." Nonsense of course, but even so you do get the feeling that a reincarnated version of yourself, minus all the cobwebs, is being allowed to wander around in an untarnished universe of limited size, where an excess of questions gets thankfully smothered in legend. No single detail is so crass as to follow you back to your contemporary present in the manner of Christianity, to which, Christian or not, you remain reluctantly bound by a thousand ties. And although it was often unbearably hot in the middle of the day, the abiding memory is of something refreshingly cool, of hours sans time spent among the mythical beasts and great superhuman kings.

WHAT DO YOU do in Persepolis? Each day you let yourself be ferried past the royal encampment that the Shah has had erected for his guests, here to celebrate the 2,500th anniversary of "his" kingdom. You climb up and down endless steps and wander around, with or without the *Guide Bleu* in your hand, depending on whether you are in an inquisitive or romantic mood. I myself prefer to call the latter wallowing, for no term describes better the rather inexact feeling which overwhelms me at such moments, causing me temporarily to abandon facts, dates, and meanings to the scholarly, and wander off over the terraces, endlessly dreaming among the wingéd beasts, kings, and colonnades, "Oh, come with old Khayyám, and leave the Wise to talk," sucking hungrily on that invisible element that at such moments, for convenience's sake, I refer to as "history," with the sun-scorched landscape far below me like an infinite collection plate. To think that "real" people have strolled here, that the endless succession of stone-carved Indians, Ethiopians, Medes, Greeks coming to pay tribute to the great king, represent real emissaries, who traveled here from all four corners of the known world on journeys that took many months. That all those lips, sealed in stone, spoke their lost languages, that their offerings had color and scent, as they themselves did. That somewhere in the center of all this, amid his stone lions and wingéd horses, his bulls and griffins, the great king was to be found, ruling the entire world, with Ahura Mazda hovering above him like Blériot in his biplane, Oh! I shall tarry a little while longer, before climbing back into the colorless cages of the New Era.

TOURISTS PHOTOGRAPH their own mortal flesh, posing among petrified time. Two government restorers are hacking away at the granite, and a sound that was also heard here three thousand years ago rings out on the dry, blistering afternoon air: iron on stone. If the Shah carries on like this, by 2500 there will be more Persepolis than there was at the time of the Battle of Nieuwpoort. And the stonemasons will be nameless once more, just like those from the time of Xerxes and Darius: a cushion of common people on which the kings have been sitting for centuries, embalmed in Xenophon and Herodotus and the sediment of legend.

Another sentiment: the mere fact that human figures, or rather figures that spring from human imagination, are carved in these reliefs, means that you feel a far greater sense of affinity with them than with the Persian art that succeeded them and preceded you; that rampant geometric ornamentation, devoid of human form. No, here—however concealed in dispassionate stylization—the kings stride out, the watchmen are vigilant, the monsters fight, and the deity takes wing.

And, however ridiculous it may sound, you know that somewhere in the middle of all this stone you yourself, insignificant latecomer though you be, are going to "happen," just as demonstrably as Darwin's ape. In the palace of Darius I, king and lion face one another in combat, like two men. Left paw of lion against right knee of king. The lion grips the left arm of the king that rests on the flowing mane. With his right, the great king thrusts his knife up to the hilt into the lion's soft underbelly.

ON THE SLOPES above Persepolis, near the grave of Artaxerxes III: six graves—the heavy doors of the tomb have been rolled back. I climb slowly. Riddle: How did they get up so high, unless they hewed the graves on the spot? I walk through the empty vault; the watchman looks as though he too is about to be swallowed up by history, vanish before my eyes. Below us the empty city of his emperors lies sweltering in the sun. The great bull stands guard at the entrance, gazing out upon the plain, the distant mountains, and all the riches the Achaemenids had dominion over. The silence that reigns here is matchless.

I stayed in Persepolis for a week. More of a sensual week than an educational one. As I said, wallowing. The light at five in the morning, the light in the afternoon, the light toward evening.

Toward the end I was visiting some of the statues at set times, as if you knew they were waiting for you. Plants and thistles flower as they do in a Grecian spring. Taking home with me the sensation others are perhaps left with after a skiing holiday, of having been in contact with something rarefied and clear.

My sensitivity to things that relate to the concept of "time" receives one last jolt when I stand in front of the royal tombs in Naqsh-i-Rustam, four kilometers from Persepolis. High up on the upper part of the mountain Kuh-i-Ho-sayn, the graves of Darius I and II, Xerxes I, and Artaxerxes are hewn. The graves themselves are cruciform, at the center a door flanked by columns, with the protomae of bulls as capitals.

Above that, the downtrodden peoples of the earth support the throne upon which the king sits, directly below Ahura Mazda, who hovers silently above it all, broad wings outstretched. Underneath the older graves, almost at eye level, are eight graves from a different dynasty, the Sassanids (AD 224–641). Thus the second row of graves was hacked out a good six hundred years after the first. The figures on these graves are rounder, more voluptuous, and a bit suppler too, than the sculptures that are positioned above them spatially, and behind them chronologically. But then I get a shock. In the second relief (Bahram II surrounded by his family) another figure is visible. He comes from a much older grave, from the third millennium, a stranger who has not been hacked away, an apparition from a time just as distant to the Sassanids as the Achaemenids are to me. A three-thousand-year-old stranger then, a five-thousand-year-old stranger now. He is as flat as a pancake, an utterly intractable fellow from an age before arms could bend, standing there like a shade, a flinty ghost, in among the suddenly almost frivolous beings who belong on my side of time. The longer I gaze at him, the less I understand him.

Now that I look at his photograph, many months later in my room, just for a moment I have that same sensation of being at too great an altitude without an oxygen mask. I can see him all right, but he cannot see me. If I went back to Naqsh-i-Rustam right now to look at him, the same thing would happen: nothing.

He is older than the oldest dynasty, he has seen them all come and go. He has the boldness of a survivor. Anyone staring at him for too long will go up in smoke.

*   *   *

SAYING SOMETHING meaningful about the political situation in Persia means going considerably further than merely ascertaining that it is an autocratic regime, to which there is little organized opposition. The permitted opposition is paid to function as it does; the "real" opposition, on the occasions when it suits the action to the word, gets imprisoned, tortured, or killed.

You do not hear much about this in Persia itself. A heavy veil of silence covers everything. Fear of the secret police, the SAVAK, predominates. The SAVAK is everywhere, at home and abroad, powerful and invisible. At the center of all the webs sits the Shah. When you compare him to other despots he appears to be considerably more enlightened, but it is questionable whether this is true. The old structures of the country are being violently overthrown, but it is unclear who is really profiting from it, and whether the country is not making the same enormous mistake that Spain made at the time of the conquistadors, when it neglected its domestic structures in favor of all that tempting gold, and to this day is still lumbered with the consequences.

The Shah is dismissive of foreign capital, but is raking it in nevertheless, along with the hoards of foreigners that go with it. In the meantime the agrarian population, the small farmers, can read the writing on the wall: 58 percent of the total population now, 25 percent later. But what will these dispossessed do? And who will cultivate the land? Shellcott, Hawaiian Agronomics, and other multinationals have already "replaced" at least seventeen thousand Persian farmers and are presently farming the land with foreign experts and tax-free imported machinery. But the yield is less than that of Persian farmers in the irrigated regions.

Why so many foreigners? Because there are so few Persians with the right qualifications. Why is this? Because the universities are dependent on the government, which regards all university activities with suspicion, stymies independent thought, has infiltrated every rank with the SAVAK, and, in a nutshell, operates according to the principle: if our own people are not good enough we will *buy* people from abroad. And so everything gets purchased, except a solid national infrastructure.

Speeches, statistics; when you walk around initially it all seems highly impressive. The Shah is intelligent, he wants the best for his people, he has started a white revolution, he wants to make Persia a big player on the world stage. And even if per capita incomes are not as high as is claimed, even if they are not rising, or not as rapidly as is reported, and even if there is extensive corruption at all levels, you still get the impression of a country that is doing well.

So what can go wrong, if it is all going so well? There are those who in answer to this question recall the ghost of Ngo Dinh Diem, former prime minister of South Vietnam, who was brought down when he was of no more use to the Americans. The Shah, restored to his throne in 1953 with the help of the CIA, is only too aware of this, even though to conjure up this specter seems irrelevant at present, when interests are running parallel. But will that always be the case? And if not, won't the opponents within the country, invisible right now, and those workers and academics who for a variety of reasons remain abroad, all at once become highly visible?

In the glow of the Persian dynastic opulence one could almost forget that this most recent dynasty is but a scratch on the great stone of history: the Shah's father was a colonel in the army that in 1921 helped to topple the ruling Qajar dynasty. And even though it is said that all officer promotions are personally vetted by the Shah, a new colonel could always be waiting in the wings. It is all speculation. Speculation which is certainly reinforced by the fear, silence, and secretiveness of the regime itself. Foreign diplomats steer carefully around such questions: no one has forgotten the vicious reprisals meted out to the Netherlands when the Shah felt personally insulted by the court case resulting from the occupation of the Persian Embassy in The Hague. According to Amnesty International there are twenty thousand political prisoners. The Shah refers only to communists, traitors, and saboteurs. According to him there are no political prisoners. That same reticence that obscures everything also makes it difficult, after one not very lengthy visit, for an outsider to judge whether the regime's foundations are solidly embedded in the popular bedrock. Something is definitely brewing in purist Muslim circles, and it is certainly also true that the tempestuous, excessively ambitious development program is stirring up forces too powerful to remain permanently under the control of one man.

MAY, JUNE 1975

Upon Her Dead Bones They Built Mantua

WHAT I AM DOING is idiotic, of course: walking out of a town only to return to it, but this is exactly what I intended. While I am walking I do not look around because if I did everything would evaporate, melt, disappear. It has to do with as if. *As if* I am emerging, on foot, from the low-lying, chilly Lombard plains, a figure in the mist. I am trying to imagine that I have been trudging through the landscape of the Mincio—Virgil's river—for a long time, and that at the end of my journey I shall see a vision, the silhouette of Mantua. I can hear my own footsteps on the low bridge. To my left and right a broad stretch of water, Lago Superiore, Lago di Mezzo. Two fishermen, like a Japanese drawing, on their boat in the haze. All is very quiet. I continue a fair way along the road to Verona. Then I become a real traveler, turn around, and approach the city of the Gonzagas.

Crenellations, towers, domes, all of it shrouded in that vague curtain of winter and the coming evening, a curtain I cannot draw aside. It moves softly, the palaces bob and float. When I reach the town I turn left and walk, still by the water, toward the Porta San Giorgio, until I am standing in front of the forbidding, deathly silent mass of the Palazzo Ducale. No sentries, no horses; in the deserted courtyard a car suddenly starts and jolts me out of the past. I can see the back of a wide flowing cloak and the theatrical gesture of a crowned head high on the baroque façade of the cathedral. In the Romanesque campanile a bell starts to toll, deep and somber, as though the invisible bell-ringer knows the sound will be muffled by the mist, and that no one will answer his summons. The square in front of the cathedral is empty, a stone piazza surrounded by high buildings. Time cannot act and history is nothing more than a collection of moments—so just how *does* one refer to the powers that preserve and at the same time alter a square like this?

THERE IS A painting by Domenico Morone dating from 1494, in which this square (now Piazza Sordello) is depicted. A picture within a picture within a picture: when, standing in this square, I think about that painting, I see an event that took place in 1328 painted 160 years later. A whirling mass of knights on horse-back fighting, the fall of the Bonacolsis, forced after a century's dominion to cede power to the Gonzagas. Dead and gone—only their names still loiter here. The Gothic façade of the cathedral has been demolished, the older, Romanesque tower that I am standing next to now has survived. In the painting the landscape is somewhat elevated—as though it is hilly—but this is a lie.

The palace of the Bonacolsis, later to become the Palazzo Ducale of the Gonzagas, appears unaltered: the same reddish, massive brick construction; the wrought-iron cages abutting the forbidding façade, the broad, square battlements outlined against the canvas of evening. I stand in all these layers of time and imagine the human screams, the sound of hooves and whin-nying horses. It must have echoed between these walls just as the bell's summons does now.

THROUGH A GATE in the sober baroque façade—it can be done—I make my way inside. The misunderstandings multiply. It must be the most worldly church I have ever seen. Long double rows of

Corinthian pillars, a forest of stone with a holy plain in between. It has nothing to do with Christianity, neither has it any of the magic of Greek temples. I find it hard to imagine that the building is old and at the same time must once have been incredibly modern—a farewell to the Gothic and consequently possessing a fantastic ambiguity. The shuttle flies back and forth here: a heathen temple for the Christian god, the banishing of a thousand years of darkness behind which was supposed to be the clear light of classical antiquity that would light up this new epoch; *Rinascimento*. I can see that it is a "beautiful" building, but it does not move me, and matters are not improved much when I pass through a narrow passageway into a tiny chapel and see two open coffins hanging on the walls. They contain corpses, tanned and shrunken, the claws with the too-long gray nails folded one over the other on top of the dingy monk's robes.

WHEN I COME again out into the evening, a hazy moon is trapped between the spliced mouth of one of the battlements. The cold from the ground seems to permeate my body, the shutters of the shops rattle as they come down, Mantua is preparing for the night. I intend to walk back to my hotel, but I lose my way in a labyrinth. The passers-by are more warmly dressed than I am, the streets narrow and gloomy. There is a wintry, unwelcoming air about the place; this is a town on a low-lying marshy plain, the north of a southern country. The cold has a free hand here—the openness, the volubility of Italy is entirely lacking. The people shut themselves up in their houses and leave the town to the stranger. I come across a tiny church and go inside. A poster hangs in the vestibule.

On December 4 the feast of the patron saints of the army will be celebrated with *particulare solennità* and the help of the fourth *Reggimento Artiglia Missili c/a*. I love my century! In front

of a confessional sits a small girl. As I pass by I glimpse the white
face of the priest and hear the ghastly, intimate whispering. She
gestures, argues, rocks back and forth in a girlish sort of way.
His waxy hands swarm toward her arms and draw gestures on
the air. She is wearing blue trousers and a short raincoat. She
appears to be pleading. Mothers and children walk in and out
of the church talking loudly, from outside comes the sound of a
souped-up moped. I remain sitting because I want to see her face,
and when she turns round I do—young, blonde, and expression-
less, someone who has wiped her sins on an old man.

TRAVELING HAS A zealousness about it that turns the traveler
into a complete blockhead. He is searching for the extraordinary within the everyday environment of others. Coming from
Amsterdam himself he would not dream in that particular city of
princes on the Prinsengracht, yet in Mantua he attaches a meaning
to names that goes far beyond everyday usage. Palazzo del Podestà,
Palazzo della Raggione, Power, Reason—it fits the image he has
of the Renaissance princes for whom he is searching. It is more
the case that the image of normality gets in the way by obscuring
the five- or six-hundred-year-old world he is trying to reach. The
actuality that surrounds him is admissible in so far as it enables
him to decide between a false portrayal of continuity and a true
one—to see the past in the present. Churches are good for this
since the very same religion is still practiced within them. Food
is perhaps even better. Sitting in a shadowy inn, with a jug of the
robust local red and a thick, ochre slice of polenta on his plate
next to a hunk of stewed wild boar, it all seems to go back way
beyond the Gonzagas and Bonacolsis to more ancient times. To
the poet who was born near this town and sang the praises of
those who worked the land here:

... at secura quies et nescia fallere vita,
dives opum variarum, at latis otia fundis,
speluncae, vivusque lacus, et frigida Tempe
mugitusque boum mollesque sub arbore somni
non absunt ...

... who still sleep without cares and live without
    deception
endowed with all manner of plenty, peaceful in the open
    countryside
in caves, lakes of living water, cool dark fens
with the raucous music of the livestock, the sweet sleep of
    afternoon
under the trees ...

Virgil, Georgics, II, 467–70

Look at him sitting there, this traveler—he is alone but not lonely, for he is playing a game. He calls the restaurant an inn, and in the faces of the other wayfarers sees gestures and personae he has seen in the paintings of Romano, Mantegna, and Pisanello. In solitary dispute at the far end of the room he hears the musical accents— undeterred by a lack of any other voices—of Tromboncino's *frottole.* It's a game, he knows it is both true and untrue, he is assembling falsehoods to make a plausible past. The game is called continuity, and contrary to what other people think he does not reject the contemporary world, but wishes to shore it up—memory and recognition being the tools. This is why he is reading the work of a poet for whom this town in each successive era has erected a new statue, up to and including the chalky-white, fascistic monument he is going to look at tomorrow. But this recognition is hard work; he has to remain blind to everything save what he is looking for, and to find what he is looking for he has acquired an extra forehead, covered in eyes. And yet it is really quite straightforward; in that real tableau in the center of the room—of pheasants, huge mushrooms, crisp green lettuce, cheeses, sides of beef, fruit, and flowers—he simply has to identify the spirit of earlier fruits, the abundance in paintings, where that same food has existed untouched for six hundred years; the round bread roll, for example, which now he breaks and eats, yet will rediscover untouched two days later at the Palazzo del Tè, it having been slipped onto the small, flower-decorated table at the banquet of the gods in the Hall of Psyche, by a devilish figure. And why should he have changed when the bread, cheese, wine, and meat have not, and the same farmers as always raise their stock, reap and sow, milk and hunt in the region surrounding this town?

Cloaked in his atavisms I go outside. Neon light, the sound of TVs from inside shuttered houses. Television, the distorted voices of people—a sound like an unattractive dialect. Once again I cannot find my way back to the hotel and do not feel like sleeping anyway. Wandering through the streets I catch sight of a stone tablet cemented on the wall. It is quite high up, the chiseled letters are not easy to decipher, only what is written underneath: *Dante, Inferno, xx-88–96*. Evidently, I am not the sole worker in the memory factory, but only when I am back home and look up the passage do I see how multilayered this memory is: somebody wants me to think of Dante and constrains me to read the passage in which Virgil, who accompanied him on his descent into the pits of hell, recalls how Mantua came into being.

The poet tells his fellow poet how Manto (*quella que ricopre le mammelle / Che non tu vedi*—she who covers her breasts / which you do not see) after much wandering comes across a plain where the water of the Mincio "spreads out and forms a marsh." She remains there and when she dies leaves her "empty body" behind (*e vi lascio suo corpo vano*) and the people who lived in those parts came together at that spot, protected by the marsh that completely surrounded it.

> *Fer la città sovra quell' ossa morte;*
> *E per colei, che 'l loco prima elesse,*
> *Mantova l'appellar senz'altra sorte.*

> Upon those dead bones they built the town
> and named it Mantua, without hesitation,
> after she who had first chosen that spot.

A strong line of poetry can become a physical sensation.

WHEN I OPEN the window of my hotel room I feel how the icy cold of the nearby water wants to get in and, worse still, that all this veiled splendor—I can see the shrouded forms above the rooftops—rests on the fragile bones of its mythical founder.

Why am I here? A month ago I was in London visiting an exhibition of Japanese art from the Tokugawa-shōgun era. At the same time in the Victoria and Albert Museum there was an exhibition about the Gonzagas, rulers of Mantua from the fourteenth until the eighteenth century. Tokugawas, Gonzagas, absolute rulers, samurai and *condottieri*, courts that aimed to acquire prestige and draw artists to them by their resplendence—something about the similarity struck me. The two exhibitions are about the rulers not the artists, but it is the art that we come to admire, not the pulverized ruler. And yet their names are inextricably bound, just like the mysterious pair of Ss on the emblem that Henry VII of

Lancaster presented to the court of the Gonzagas. The faces of the Gonzagas were more familiar to me than those of the Tokugawas, but the wide, monumental court dress of Tokugawa Iewasu was redolent of the very same thing as the strange garb—partially armor-clad, and encrusted with rising moons—of Vincenzo I, fourth Duke of Mantua, painted in vain and steely silence by Pourbus: *power*.

POWER AS A MEANS to art, art as a means to power; it applies to other Renaissance princes as well, but the Gonzaga family—not in fact so very rich, and not always particularly artistic either—were able to use it to optimal advantage. Their family tree was displayed at the beginning of the exhibition. Those things sometimes remind me of a map of a huge but unfamiliar city's underground railway system. The line begins somewhere in an obscure northern suburb, diverges, extends in every direction, and ends, sad and lonely on a run-down south-eastern estate: Ferdinando Gonzaga (1650–1708), tenth Duke. Between him and Luigi, the first *capitano*, lies a chess-board of carefully arranged events, advantageous marriages, and cardinals' hats. Beside it hangs another chart, the kind that yanks you into the past on a magic towing hook. Meanwhile, in the center the Gonzagas stream on, overflowing like a watercourse into one another's names and ever grander titles. To the right and left of their line lie the mountain chains of contemporary events: Copernicus's theories, the Pazzi plot that set out in vain to put a stop to the rule of the Medicis in Florence, Luther and his ninety-five theses, Shakespeare's birth—concluding with the narrow pass of Galileo's telescope and the clearance sale of the entire collection of Gonzaga treasures to Charles I, just before Mantua was invaded and plundered for the first time in its history. Cromwell squandered part of the loot by selling it overseas, and in so doing blew the centuries-old collection, which was an artwork in itself, to smithereens. The gems—Titian, Mantegna, Rubens—were stolen from the necklace and scattered through the museums of the world. What remained was the idea, and this was well illustrated at the exhibition. Within a fairly small space a brilliant decor designer had recreated parts of the ducal palace, there were photo-reconstructions, scale models, and a huge number of medals, engravings, manuscripts, books, letters, musical scores (Palestrina, Monteverdi), ceramic tiles (a sunburst with the motto *per un exir*, for a desire, and a muzzle with the motto *cautius*, more careful), Nicolà da Urbino's wonderful, vividly colored bowls, wooden, bronze, and marble sculptures and paintings of the Gonzagas themselves; a somber-looking clan, plagued by hereditary arthritis, with broad, rough-featured faces, thick lips, slightly bulging eyes, and massive square chins that give notice of power.

IT IS A MONTH later now. An audio-visual display at the exhibition has lured me to Mantua at the wrong time of year—the image of water, quiet surfaces of polished steel, taken from the top of a tower in the Palazzo Ducale. The chemistry of memory reflected back another image, a hot summer in Amsterdam years ago during the annual Holland Festival; leaving the Nicolaaskerk after an evening of Monteverdi's madrigals, walking by the quiet water of the Prins Hendrikkade. I was thinking about Venice because back then I associated Monteverdi with it. Now I know that *Orfeo* was in fact first performed in Mantua, in 1607, at the court of the Gonzagas—not in a city intersected by water, but in a citadel surrounded by it. Which is why I am sitting here in my hotel room, listening to the bells of San Andrea sounding the twelfth hour and being glad for once that walls and glass cannot keep out that sound.

I can only think about the past irrationally, or rather, only in a chaotic, paradoxical fashion that proves nothing, yet I know that it was that thick-lipped, big-headed family of horse breeders and opportune marriage-makers who summoned me here across the water: the "insatiable collector" Isabella d'Este; the pious hunchback Guglielmo; Federico, who bought 130 Flemish landscapes in one day and wanted to be buried *sine pompa aut cerimonia*; Vicenzo, who wanted to be placed upon his bier in a sitting position and buried on a marble throne (*sedendo super cathedra marmorea*); Francesco, the fourth *capitano* who had his wife Agnese Visconti beheaded for adultery; Ludovico who after endless negotiations managed to get the grumpy Mantegna to travel to Mantua in 1460, where he remained for the rest of his life. This cavalcade of knights who bartered their military prowess and their horses to third parties, no family of geniuses this, and not really rulers of extensive territories either, more a line of patrons who augmented their name with that of the artists whom they bought with borrowed money and encouraged and spurred on, so that in some obscure and unthinkable "later" their name would adorn an exhibition in London, the city that Francesco visited in 1389 *ad videndum partes illas*, "with the intention of seeing those parts."

The mist is still there. Tendrils of it hang about the stalls of cheeses, sausages, and dried fish near the church of San Andrea. Inside the church it is dark—it feels more like the final moments of daylight than the first. I walk forward into the heart of Alberti's finely honed perspectival space. The lofty barrel vaulting is stopped in its tracks by the cupola, which from the outside I had not imagined to be so large. Suddenly the half-circle I can see from where I am standing slices through the looming mass of the vaulting with geometric precision, and that feeling you never have in a Romanesque church, only in a Renaissance building, comes over me: that *you yourself* are the gauge by which the space is meas-ured. That lines could be (or *are* being) drawn from your person to every imaginable point within that space. Accordingly you become, besides an enthralled spectator, a mechanically moving object—a split sensation that once heralded the coming of a new era more clearly than any words were able to express.

In the Palazzo Ducale a frozen group is waiting for the conducted tour. You are not allowed in on your own and the guide's tempo is inhuman. A ragbag of visual impressions is tipped over us: we let ourselves be shunted up staircases, around rooms, halls, and galleries, but even on the second and third time none of it sticks, the haste increases the transience. I see my own familiar face flitting past in the clouded mirrors like a ghost, let myself be led carefully up the staircase with the worn steps, which the guests used to clamber up, horse and all! I crouch obediently in the tiny, myste-rious dwarfs' rooms, and look out over the water to the shrouded flatlands beyond. I hang back when we come to Pisanello's frescos, discovered not so long ago after staying concealed for hundreds of years. Curious, something that is unfinished but old nevertheless, in a strange way the very opposite of a ruin. I gaze at those markings and lines that have remained on the walls, the portrayal of a cruel battle. A knight is lying on his back, deathly still in the midst of the violence, an upturned human tank, helpless in his metal carcass. A long, delicate hand rests limp on the metal armor, the vulnerability of faces discernible behind open visors, others stay hidden behind bird-like iron beaks. Translucent as they are, almost floating upon those huge walls, the lightly sketched figures nevertheless exude a powerful stench of struggle and death.

The most memorable is still the *Camera degli Sposi*, or *Camera Picta*. It took Mantegna nine years to complete. His patrons thought this too long, but they were wrong. Nine years is not long for the creation of a cosmos, for that is what it is. Upon the few square meters of wall within that room Mantegna has fashioned an entire world, in which the reality of the Gonzagas is portrayed within the sensual deceit of the newly discovered perspective. Women and putti look down at you from the open heavens over a balustrade even as you look up. One of these tiny angels is holding Newton's russet apple in his hand, which is about to come down and hit you. The figures in the mural stand up straight, turned toward each other strangely and hieratically. Each is gazing elsewhere, their expressions all of total seriousness; they knew they would be inhabiting this room for all time. The refinement of the painter is phenomenal: the dog's paw, for example, which he paints hanging just over the dado so that it is as though the creature is about to spring into the room. You stand there dazzled by so much brilliance, and at the same time there is the fear that suddenly it will all come to a stop; threatening curtains hang everywhere, pushed aside, billowing out, blowing in the invisible breeze, painted in such a way that it seems that an evil hand might easily draw them shut again, pitching the prince and his court and that spacious antique landscape with its diminutive hunters and peasants back into an untraceable limestone grave of lost time.

ON MY WAY OUT, I buy a postcard showing a labyrinthine ceiling displaying the motto of Duke Vicenzo. *"Forse che si, forse che no"* is painted in golden letters on the myriad blue paths, and because it does not end anywhere it appears to have been written a thousand times. "Perhaps, perhaps not." Protected by this talisman I end where I began and walk back along the road to where I will be able to see the dream-like vision—behind a cloak of mist that is slowly drawn across.

1983

Zurich

ON MY WAY to Zurich somebody got there ahead of me, a sculptor who also paints and draws. His name is Winter, and he has altered the city I know. His materials are snow, ice, mist, early nightfall, cold. His work takes some getting used to, it is fairly strong stuff. And he must have toiled like one possessed; the faces of the living, the graves of the dead, the color of the water suddenly so much darker, he has left his mark everywhere. Neither has he spared the efforts of his colleagues, all over the place I see remodeling, additions, and corrections.

The effect of all this is sometimes quite bizarre. I do not know whether this applies to everyone who travels a lot, but all over the world I have stone friends whom I look up whenever I am in town. In Paris there is Montaigne in the rue des Écoles, in London—on the banks of the Thames—the Sphinx; in León the sleeping bishop in a corner of the cathedral; and in Zurich the two serious, chaste, contemplative female figures on each side of the fountain on Rämistrasse. These sculptures do not have anything in common, they do not know one another, but each one inspired a particular thought or memory that caused me to pause next to them. And now I feel that I know them personally, that I would like to talk to them and see how they are.

Anyone who thinks this is odd should ask himself just what those statues are doing there. By and large to remind us of something we might otherwise forget, although not, I suspect, in the case of these two women by the fountain. They are here to keep us company, to tell us something that is not immediately definable, something to do with femininity and beauty, with contemplation. Something, at any rate, to give you pause on your way from the Kunsthaus to the Kronenhalle or to the shores of Lake Zurich, even if only to say hello.

I am fond of these two statues. I have known them in summer and in autumn. They may not be exceptional, but they exude a melancholic earnestness that always makes me want to lay my hand on an arm for a moment, and each time I do the hard, gritty texture of their skin amazes me, as if I had actually expected the skin to be smooth, warm, and alive, matching their youth. But what sort of paradox is this? If these were real women I would not dare touch them, not only because touching strangers is something you do not do, but also because the limestone of their breasts and shoulders would then have been swiftly transformed into the roughness and flakiness of a skin disease, whereas that very same limestone beneath my hand now feels so agreeable, implying both youth and luster.

THE ARTIST IS A deceiver, we know this, it is the reason Plato could not stand the genus. But a relationship with a statue must surely be reckoned among the secret desires, especially now that other artist, Winter, has shown an interest in my two lady friends. He has laid snow in their laps, and on their hair and shoulders, as if, in spite of his being the embodiment of cold, the sight of their soft naked-ness on these frozen days is unbearable to him. They themselves do not appear in the least bothered by it, but carry on thinking their slow thoughts, seemingly unaware of the fluffy white cape, just as they also continue to stare right through me at the ground.

Something else concerns them, the absence of the water perhaps, which normally streams through their stony silence. Winter has sculpted a polished diamond of ice at the mouth of the fountain; tiny, soft snowflakes alight delicately upon it and then appear to vanish. I must extricate myself from this intimacy.

"White soot," "minced feathers," is how the Dutch writer Constantijn Huygens once described snow, and covered in this white soot and those feathers I cross Bellevueplatz toward the water. Here too Winter has been busy, but this time as a Chinese watercolorist who has left his colors at home. Near the bridge stone steps lead down to the water, but I stay a while leaning against the balustrade. Below me is an Iranian woman in a blue silk headscarf. She has three children with her and is about to cast bread to the waterfowl, using the age-old gesture of the sower (which we will soon recognize only from paintings).

Amazing: it seems Zeno's law holds sway here—the duration of that grand sweeping action being broken down into an endless series of separate moments, and no matter how far away the swans, gulls, coots, and ducks are, their computers have already registered this emblematic signal; now it is all down to whoever reaches the airborne bread first. The swans bear down like battle-ships, followed by an entire flotilla of tinier paddling craft. The gulls carry out their attack from the air, feathered fighter planes, screaming like a choir of demented old women.

How does nature deal with this sort of thing? In the time it takes a swan neck to reach down to the water, a humble moorhen will already have the piece of bread in its beak, that is, so long as a gull has not intercepted it on the wing. It is always difficult to avoid the conclusion that some sort of racial or social pecking order is being reflected here. But these are human notions. We find a swan more beautiful or aristocratic than one of those

Sancho Panza moorhens, but how do they see it? Do ducks bear grudges toward swans? Are coots grimly resentful of seagulls? Or is it purely a thrashing, quacking, scrabbling, screeching determination to survive? Is there sadness when they mis-grab for the umpteenth time, and are conclusions then drawn? You see how people struggle with this, desperately trying to direct toward a far corner the brown duck which just cannot get a break, to increase its chances, and their frustration too when at the last moment one of those mongrels from the gull mafia makes off with the caviar.

PATHÉTIQUE: six swans in a circle all performing their arabesque at the same time because Pavlov says so, and then raising those long necks, once again simultaneously—a bouquet fit to tie a ribbon around. In the distance two small boats, fishermen. The Chinese master needed two, perhaps three, brush strokes to capture it. For the opposite shore of the lake he has selected a broader brush, but has washed the ink with water afterward. What is left would prefer to present itself as nothingness, but the master is too sophisticated for that; he has been making these drawings for thousands of years after all, and has made the far side disappear into itself, something with only the hint of nothingness.

TIME AND BRONZE, strange kin, but in cities like this the one is unthinkable without the other. Apparently there was once no time, and after that a long period when no one was around to notice it, let alone measure it. All this was not the reason for the invention of bronze, but once it had been these people who were able to make bells with it. Sleep and dozing are imitations of that timeless age. (Without the word *time* hardly anything can be expressed.) The first bronze chime spills into the silent nothingness, like a sign for rebirth. It is time to live, but not quite yet. First count them. Two light, bronze chimes. An attempt to measure the immeasurable. Half of four, but which four? It is dark in my quiet room; the night wants me back and I am willing. Three now, adding an element of place, it must be the Grossmünster, I recognize the sound.

So now I am both in time and in space and belong to the world of man. Three-quarters of one hour or another have passed. Now I must wait one more quarter of an hour. Then the bronze will count to four, after which will come the proper, deeper toll, then another, and another. Only when I have counted all of them can I chart my position, like a ship on the ocean. Five, says the bronze, as it has done for centuries. I am bound by the threads of that sound to the invisible strangers who are listening too. Five. Six. Seven. Eight. Predigerkirche, Fraumünster, tenor, baritone, bass, they are all trying to say the same thing, but they let one another go first; simultaneity is for computers, not for the mortals for whom the bell tolls. But not yet. I get up.

It is still snowing, a bright, shining city. I will don it like an article of clothing, with all its names and treasures, its centuries-old mutterings, with what I see and know and what I shall never know, with its public and private memories. People tend to forget it, but cities converse unremittingly, and cities like this one have been doing so for perhaps more than a thousand years. There is always somebody speaking, whispering, shouting, arguing, preaching, judging, consoling, seducing, counting, confessing, complaining. It has never really been silent, and all those words cling to the walls like material things, patina, varnish. Impossible to remove, audible only to the sharpest ears, those of the saunterer, the man who wanders through the labyrinth of alleyways, their names surrounding him like a liquid element—Rindermarkt, Froschgasse, Spiegelgasse, Münstergasse—until he is standing in the shadow of the big building from where the old emperor in his golden crown looks down upon the river. Always that same flowing water continuously imitating the flow of time, a sound heard here long before people arrived.

* * *

GROSSMÜNSTER. It was once a Catholic church. Converted churches, can you say that? I feel a certain apprehension, disorientation. A long time ago, due to an administrative error my sister and I, having been evacuated from The Hague in wartime, were placed in what we call a *School met den Bijbel* (School of the Good Book) in eastern Holland. This did not last long, for on the very first day the other children copped on to the fact that we were "papists" and chased us across the playground into a corner where they spat in our faces. This has not left me with a trauma, but neither have I forgotten it. We refer to the rigidly orthodox type of Protestantism practiced in those parts as the *zwartekousenkerk* (church of the black stockings). As far as I know its members are to this day not allowed to watch television; in districts where they hold the majority there is no swimming on Sundays, and some of them even refuse to have their children vaccinated against polio, because to do so one would be interfering with the mysterious workings of God.

Does this lie at the root of my slight apprehension? I wonder. No, of course not, but even so the cold sternness of this building does have an alien feel about it. At the spot where the altar should be a tall Christmas tree now stands, entirely devoid of decoration, a heathen symbol that probably has no idea what it is doing here, apart from filling an empty space. A Christmas tree without lights is a *displaced person*; it stands there doing its best to be a tree, but would presumably rather have done this in a wood. I go and

sit near it, in one of the choir stalls, which also confuse me. They
are obviously not old, so why have they been put here? In the past,
benches like these were meant for the monks or canons while
they floated psalms back and forth to one another, something you
still see on feast days in cathedrals, and daily in the monasteries of
such contemplative orders as the Trappists and the Benedictines.
I feel more at home higher up, where are the inaccessible, stony
heaven arches, unconcerned with the alterations the living
have brought about down below. And the capitals, too, speak a
language familiar to me from Romanesque churches in Lombardy
and Aragon, mythical beasts, oriental floral motifs, geometrical
decoration, the visual language of the Middle Ages.

Yet it remains chilly, austere; the gray hardness of the high,
empty walls brooks no diversion, no human forms, no escape
route for distracted thoughts like mine: the Word is the sole
occupant here, something no writer could object to, surely?
Even so, as I wander slowly toward the front until directly beneath
the far more recent, colorful windows by Augusto Giacometti,
all at once I see two headless shades who seem to be walking
toward me through a thick mist, keen to tell me the story of their
martyrdom. Regula and Felix; they are ashen now, and carry
their chopped-off heads under their arms as if still meaning to
take them somewhere. Their clothes may have faded, but their
legend has remained. They belonged to a Roman legion from
Egyptian Thebes, sent to Wallis in the far north to fight against the
Christians. But these legionaries were themselves Christian, and to
avoid having to kill their brothers in faith fled to Turcium, where
they were condemned by the governor Decius and beheaded on
an islet in the Limmat. (Beheading seems to be linked to water in
this city—the powerful Hans Waldmann was also conveyed by
ship to his place of execution.)

I cannot decide whether or not I like this church. The Catholic in me misses the colorful and feminine, the theatrical, but visiting the ascetic building for a second time the following Sunday I have another opportunity to reflect upon it. The apprehension is still there, but that may be because I have never attended a Protestant church service before. The words *Geld und Geist* (money and mind) inadvertently come to me as I accompany the staunch burghers within. This is the title of a fascinating book about Zurich by Gordon Craig, which I am reading at present, and whose title keeps popping into my head.

Friends who live here have led me to understand that it makes a huge difference who is preaching, which is hardly surprising in a church where the Word takes centre stage. Rather, what I found strange—and perhaps my solemn fellow churchgoers did too—was the sermon's theme, taken from Tobit, one of the books of the Apocrypha, the story of poor Tobias who is to wed Sarah. The problem is that Sarah has done this seven times before, but all her husbands have died on their wedding night, before the marriage had been consummated. Tobias has fallen in with a traveling companion along the way (an angel, though he does not know this) who counsels him to burn the heart and liver of a fish as an offering to God on arriving at his betrothed's house. He does this, the marriage is accomplished (in every respect), and Sarah's father who has already had the grave of the next victim dug, can have it filled in again. Tobias's burnt offering has caused the murderous demon that had possessed Sarah to flee to the farthest corner of Egypt, the traveling companion reveals himself to be the archangel Raphael, and the clergyman is faced with a dilemma—for the gap between burnt offering and incense is but a slender one, and incense has of course no place in this church, "where Zwingli himself preached against such pagan practices."

The congregation around me, sixty-odd earnest citizens, look up, as I do, at the imposing man (handsome face, white bands, black gown, with something of a Swedish star from a Bergman film about him), in expectation of which side he will come down on. He proceeds to tell us that recently, together with his wife (a small shock runs through me, the taboo still runs deep), he visited a young, alternative healer. I realize where this is leading: God helps us, when it pleases Him, in unexpected ways. Just for a moment I have a subversive fantasy in which the bronze doors creak slowly open and Zwingli enters, with the thunderous footsteps of the Stone Guest, demanding that the clergyman explain this untimely defense of an odor long since driven from the building. But then the man in the pulpit exhorts us to pray for people in need, for victims of war, and finally for animals and plants too. Suddenly I see blades of glass, fir trees, cactuses, rainforest, oaks, and those gigantic, thousand-year-old trees along the American Pacific coast. The organ showers us with Pachelbel, the congregation embarks ever so softly upon Hymn 282 (*"Wer nun den lieben Gott lässt walten"*), and accompanied by animals, plants and humans I sing along as well as I can, resolving to look up the animals in their snow-bound zoo later this week, although I harbor a secret suspicion that it would make more sense if the plants and animals in their bewildering state of innocence prayed for us, rather than the other way round.

When I re-emerge it is still quiet in Zurich. The money is sleeping in the banks, the computers are speculating *Beyond Good and Evil*, the tram in which I travel to the Landesmuseum is all but empty. There is music at the museum too, a choir of young people singing polyphonic medieval music: a cappella, Desprez, Ockeghem, it is like coming home. The small space in which they are singing is full up, it is standing room only. I find myself in two

Middle Ages at once, in front of me the choir of young men and women in their bright red blouses, and behind me a room in late-medieval style, with the city's arms in stained glass. *Lamentatio, missa orationum*, the plaintive, inwardly torn soul resonates in music, which is anything but torn, a tissue of sounds constantly drawing near and departing from one another, sound that has remained pristine because it refused to incorporate the world's decay, the voices sound virginal, unsullied, as though not of this world but already part of that other one.

THE MUSEUM ITSELF is an endless treasure trove; I wander for hours, absorbed in the history of this city and country. Two-headed eagles, ancient blazons of a vanished aristocracy, correspondence from *gar alten Kriegen* (many an old war), the Rathhausstube von Mellingen (the ceremonial chambers of Mellingen Town Hall) dating from 1467, lances, and *Minnekästchen* (cabinets in which wedding bans were posted), an abbess's slippers, Zwingli's Bible, the knights and poets of the Manessische literary circle. I proceed unhurriedly through the centuries, a thousand-year-old man lost in his memories. His? No, of course not, and yet, what is a museum if not a collective memory in which you are able to participate by walking around in it?

Five centuries on, Waldmann's gold chain is still as dazzling as when he was forced to relinquish it, the face behind its closed, atavistic vizier remains concealed, Katherine von Zimmer's room is one I have been in so many times already, or dreamed I had, and of course I still remember what the city looked like in 1627.

How to choose from such profusion? You do not of course, you just get caught up by something, the delightful or grotesque, images which will return to you in your dreams. "The Emperor Galerius decrees that the tongue of the Holy Romanus be cut off"—a press photograph from 1420. The Emperor pivots on long,

tapering feet, as if the scene has nothing to do with him. With one hand he is pointing into the adjacent panel, where a soldier in a golden tunic, wielding a substantial knife, has just knelt down in order to reach his victim more easily. The holy man in his cloak of many folds sits half turned toward him—it makes for easier chopping. He is far bigger than the soldier, his closely shaven head is lifted up toward his executioner, his tongue stuck out as far as possible. Ockeghem's translucent music is suddenly very far away, not wanting to be associated with the bloody scream that will follow in a second's time.

The Last Supper, which hangs in the same room, dates from a hundred years later. Time differences are the prerogative of the living, at least they are when it concerns the past. Lindenholz, the Rheinau Monastery, 1510. The apostles are arranged so chaotically that I count them to see whether in fact there are twelve. (Absurd this, a bit like counting your change at a vending machine—it is always right.) The dish on the table is upended toward us, rather like Daniel Spoerri's paintings. Strange, bearded faces. The bread on the table is of gold, there is a dead animal in the dish, the head separated from the carcass, one front paw stretched over the rim, as if the creature is still sleeping. The apostle seated literally in the right-hand corner of the scene cuts the golden bread. His neighbor places his right hand almost tenderly upon the dead animal's flank, in his left he holds aloft a Coburg loaf. I still know what these images signify, the Last Suppers, crucifixions, madonnas and child, annunciations, all estranged from their original contexts, removed from monasteries and churches and tidied away in secular surroundings. Art, no longer to be knelt in front of. Art, for the enjoyment only of those who still understand, becoming in all probability a few centuries on as transparent and obscure as Venus, Apollo, or Hermes, a pulchritude that no longer has any resonance.

A TRAVELER IN Zurich. He has a meal in the Kronenhalle and thinks obligatory thoughts about Joyce and *Ulysses*, he is given a guided tour of the Zentralbibliothek, including the basement rooms deep under ground, where he is shown the *Neue Zürcher Zeitung* from the day and year of his birth (July 31, 1933)—Lady in possession of modest fortune and even more to come . . . Roosevelt's New Deal, the Australian economic situation, Communist organizations in Germany under investigation, first telephone link to Colombia—and has a sense of just how long he has been alive, and then again, when the librarian deposits Vesalius and Paracelsus on the desk in front of him, how very short a time. He drinks mulled wine in the Opfelchammer, where he can still hear the voices of Böcklin and Keller, attends a concert given by the Oberwalliser Spillet (Upper Valais Minstrels) at the opera house, letting himself be enchanted and emerging floating on air, sees the madness of an Austrian curiosa collection (*Wunderkamer*), the classical simplicity of Baumgarten's photographs in the Kunsthaus—and then suddenly it is enough, enough paintings, monsters, people, voices, coats of arms, psalms, books, it is time for some peace and quiet, and where better than among the snow and animals, the plants and the dead?

I had read something about the three mightiest trees in Zurich in the book *Zuricher Baumgeschichten*. It seemed simple enough, all I had to do was go there. A tram, a stroll, and a mountain slope would bring me face to face with *Acer campestre*, the maple I already knew quite a bit about. If I were to soak its bark in vinegar it would protect me against snake bites and wound infections. If

I fermented its leaves I could survive a famine. Farmers called it *Massholder*, after the old High German *Mazzalta*, meaning "nourishment," and because it would never be part of a whole forest it had been christened *Beiläufer* (bystander), a name I found oddly appealing.

Now it was simply a question of finding it. By way of a steep, snow-covered road I had suddenly and mysteriously left the city behind, which now lay silent far below me. A man with a wheelbarrow full of dung crosses my path, cows are mooing, I pass an orchard with young fruit trees in their winter cladding, hear the wail of an ambulance from those far-off misty depths, and consider that my tree is also called the *Klangbaum* (sound tree), because its wood is used to make violins. But where is it? I pass by the beautiful, serene Jewish cemetery and know I am getting near, but the dead, beneath their impressive, snow-covered tombstones, will not say where it is, and none of the living I come across have ever heard of it. A brook babbles, as it has done since Wordsworth's day (before that brooks were seen and not heard!), but the water is not giving the tree's secret away either.

How can you tell a maple without its leaves? By the Doric fluting, according to my book, but snow-covered wood and antique marble do not really bear much resemblance to one another, and the trees all seem to be laughing at me until, lo and behold, I am standing before the only one it can be, because it is not laughing. When I rest my hand on its age-old, deeply furrowed bark I hear how, deep down under the snow, the snakes slither fearfully away. I stand there, the complete village idiot, gazing up at the tremendous tangle of deathly quiet, bare branches above me. *I am taking it in*; such expressions exist for a reason, and if I stand here long enough it will take me in too, a man with a notebook who does not come up even to its ankles. When a gust of wind got up, the tree threw some snow down on me, and from the dry rasp of its branches it seemed to be trying to say something, but whatever it was, I failed to understand it.

Its older brother, *Quercus robur*, was yet more difficult to find. A minibus, a bus, and a tram, the snowy plain of the *Allmend "unter dem Albisgütl."* That is as may be, but the people have grown decadent, they no longer know where to find the trees in which their ancestors believed the gods lived. Even though this mighty oak is apparently twenty meters high, with a spread of some six meters, even though Gottfried Keller himself painted it in watercolor, and drummer boys practiced in its shade, despite all this, neither the jogging toothpaste advert, nor the lady with her dog, nor the two old gentlemen discussing the theological niceties of original sin, know where this old idol is situated. It takes me hours to find it, but when finally I do it utterly bowls me over, its craggy, broadly spreading branches trace a Caspar David Friedrich against the suddenly coppery evening sky; of course a god used to dwell here, and no friendly specimen either, rather one with a soul of ice, a spirit of winter, a body of wood. Groaning, the oak holds sway over the landscape and listens disdainfully to the obscene whispers of the autobahn.

*   *   *

The following day the animals and the dead give me less of a hard time. I do not know whether it is due to the sun and the misty haze, but the graveyard near the zoological gardens has something light-hearted about it, as if the dead are lying there under the ground humming softly. I follow the sign that says "James Joyce," and discover that the poet has adapted himself to the prevailing mood of well-being. He sits relaxed on his chair, without an overcoat, as if he has not noticed the snow-laden spruces towering above his head. Book in hand, he is about to light another cigarette, his head buzzing with the words of many languages; his wife has stayed at home, his family is waiting below with a cup of tea. Even at this early hour he has already had a few visitors, their diffident steps imprinted in the fresh snow, each footstep a book that has been read, blending five meters further along into a different book, at the spot where Canetti's spirit realm begins. Wind, words, wind, but the thinker sleeps on beneath his simple wooden cross, he is not quite at home yet, or perhaps, like me, he can hear the distant howling of the wolves in the zoo.*

There it is just as deserted as the graveyard. People who visit the zoo on a winter's day are different, something the animals are perfectly aware of. At last we can take a good long look at one another. I talk about arthritis with the elderly lion, depression with the llama, the old times "when things were better" with the eagle, our failing memory with the snowy owl, the advantages and disadvantages of exile with an enormous elephant playfully hurling dry branches about, and all of us hear the high-pitched, compulsive, terrifying howling of the wolves, whose rendering of "Winter in Siberia" is so realistic that one can picture the sleds racing over the tundra, and hear the crack of the driver's whip. They are fine creatures, these wolves. They know their parts by heart, raise their heads heavenward, and wail their unforgettable arias. The third one, its head pointing downward, whines a low, tuneless, staccato counterpoint.

Now that there are so few of my own species around, I realize how much we belong here. After all, the front of the bars is made of the same material as the back. Surely one zoo in the world should have the courage to draw the ultimate conclusion about

---

* Canetti had then only recently died. The catholic cross was preliminary—and is now replaced by a tombstone with his signature engraved on it.

our ancestry? A cage with *Homo sapiens* in all its varying forms, perhaps then we would understand ourselves better. The question of course is whether the other animals would approve of it.

FINAL DAY. The water has been exerting a pull all week; I am keen to visit that nothingness that claims to be the other side, so I take the boat to Kilchberg. The lake is as polished as onyx, transparent daggers of ice hang from the mooring posts by the jetty, my only fellow passengers are a frozen Japanese couple, but they are not, as I am, bound for the house of Conrad Ferdinand Meyer.

The door is open, there is nobody about, perhaps the writer has gone for a stroll. I hesitate a while before entering his study. Something is wrong here, the desk is too tidy. The books on the shelves are keeping quiet (those soft pleadings to be taken out again are only audible to writers). A volume of Corneille lies on the table, did he choose it? I flip open a page in someone's diary: "5 March 1847. Have done no work." Sounds familiar! The letters of the Emperor Charles v. The memoirs of Anne of Austria. Pascal's *Pensées*. And on the wall a portrait of the master of the house dating from 1887, a stout old party in a hat, his eyes in shadow. Just for a moment he seems to be poking his tongue out at this curious, posthumous colleague who is wandering uninvited through his house. "You'd be better off reading me," he seems to be saying. "If it's me you're looking for, I'm in my books."

*   *   *

I RECEIVE THE same message half an hour later in the small churchyard where Thomas Mann lies buried. *Not at Home*, the massive block of basalt says sternly. Here too there are footsteps. Readers search out dead writers. Perhaps it is the snow making it all so severe, but they lie here unrelenting, secure within their names, Thomas Mann, Katja Mann. They are the only ones standing upright; Erika, Monika, and Michael lie at the foot of the block, small plaques in the ground, in the shade of their overwhelming parents. Someone has wiped away the snow with his hands, uncovered their names, which seem to say: "We were there too, we were there too."

And now? My Zurich days are at an end. I pack my new treasures into my suitcase: the postcards with Chagall's windows, the catalogue of the Zentralbibliothek, Zwingli pensive in profile in his Erasmus bonnet, against a blue background, the tortured bodies of ten thousand knights, the medieval painting of the martyrdom of the city's patron saints in which Zurich is still so tiny and the hills surrounding it so green; sculptures, fragments, books, memories, poems, stories, all will accompany me through the air from one ancient city to that other one, where my home is.

2002

Moonscape Mali

I T IS NIGHT-TIME on November 19, 1968. The *Général Soumaré*, a converted West German pleasure boat, moves along the still, black Niger. During the rainy season she is used as a passenger ship, plying between the capital, Bamako, and the towns of Mopti, Timbuktu, Koulikoro, and Gao, a journey of some weeks. Despite the hour, all the passengers are awake. They are either standing against the rail or sitting by the tiny portholes of their cabins listening to transistors, or rather to the silence emanating from them. While life goes on in the rest of the world, presidents turn over in their beds and the first morning papers roll off the presses in Europe, a slow, silent revolution is taking place in Mali, a country whose location is a mystery to most people, a hot, parched, penniless African republic, bigger than France and Germany combined, and consisting principally of sand. For the silent men on board the *Général Soumaré* are no ordinary passengers, and the tense group waiting on the quayside at Koulikoro, sixty kilometers from the capital, is no ordinary reception party. This is the last night of Modibo Keïta's presidency, and he knows it, and his followers on board know it, and the soldiers waiting on the quayside know it, and the fourteen officers who have bided their time under constant risk of death, they know it too. In just a short while, with that swiftness characteristic of the tropics, the curtain of night will be drawn back to reveal the world. And this is how it looks: dry, with precious little compassion for man or beast, brown, like the waters of the river; a mud-colored snake stretched listlessly in the bare savannah. But before daybreak the transistors start to crackle. The men on the ship hear it, as do those on the quayside, and anyone else in the country who is already awake. The plucking of a stringed instrument—a melody everyone recognizes—and then a voice that everyone knows too, that of the blind singer Banzoumana, banned for years, for singing about the coming of a day when the mighty would perish. Wondrous tales are told in Mali about his instrument. It can fly, and when Banzoumana sleeps it plays by itself. A sign has been given and everyone is aware of it.

IT IS THE END of an era. Like Guinea, Mali went its own way. It wanted nothing to do with the French community and the French-backed Central African franc, and became estranged from its traditional trading partners in the process. It plumped for a fervent and doctrinaire socialism, becoming alienated from its neighbors. Modibo Keïta, one of the revered founding fathers of African independence, president of the impossible Senegal–Mali–Guinea federation, which had died of anaemia back in 1962, a one-time humble schoolteacher who took the fast track, by way of prison, the vice presidency of the French National Assembly and a spell as a French minister of state, to the top job in one of the poorest countries in the world, has come to the end of the line. The guard of honor on the quayside gives the presidential salute. The populace cheers. The president returns the salute and moves toward his car. The flag is saluted, hands are shaken. Ten kilometers further on, the long black car with its red, yellow, and green flag is halted by a Russian tank. A diminutive lieutenant in paramilitary uniform approaches the president, takes him by the arm, and escorts him to a truck.

That same afternoon Lieutenant Moussa Traoré announces over the country's thirty thousand radio sets that the regime has fallen. Mali, independent for less than ten years, a country of four million souls, 4,500 private vehicles, £79 gross annual income per head, 7 dentists, 108 doctors, and 4,640 telephones, with a debt of 120 billion Malinese francs—thirty-two billion to Russia, twenty-six to France, twenty-three to Red China, seven to Egypt, six to Ghana. One Malinese franc is .01 French franc. The country is teetering on the brink of bankruptcy, trade has all but ceased, the shops in the marketplace are empty. Driven further and further toward the left by the Chinese faction within his party, the Union Soudanaise, but forced by a shortage of raw materials, an excess of stifling bureaucracy, and the discouragement of practically all foreign investment and technical know-how into a tragic cycle of impotence, fresh loans, and new, ever more unpopular measures, Keïta decides, in 1967, in defiance of the diehards in the Chinese faction, once more to make economic overtures to France. But even the 50 percent devaluation that this entails cannot save the ship of state. Under the influence of blind dogma, fraud, and the huge dissatisfaction of both the agrarian and urban population (no more millet, no tea, gasoline, cement, or money), it sinks deeper and deeper. By now parliament has long since been dissolved, opposition leaders have been murdered in suspicious circumstances, and even China cannot, or will not, provide the cash needed to keep the economy afloat. The army consists of three thousand men. It has Russian weapons, Russian tanks, Russian instructors. Its officers have been trained in France, complemented, ironically enough, by experience in the field in Algeria and Indo-China. The senior officers are of exemplary loyalty, not so much to the president as to their own position. The generation below them poses more danger, but Keïta cannot do without a good professional army because of his occasional difficulties with the fierce, independent, and aggressive Tuareg, from the north and east. Lords and masters of their own Sahara domains, they have scant respect for the black population of a state with invisible frontiers, which in their eyes hardly exists, and have to be put in their place from time to time. But it will be the army that shatters the power of the president, and the young lieutenants play their parts well. Of humble origins, serving in various garrisons the length and breadth of this vast country, they become aware of the huge discontent, the passive aversion, the contradiction of empty stomachs and hollow phrases. They set out on a slow game of poker between the possible outcomes (not excluding certain death in the event of failure) and their own nationalistic impatience. They are not antisocialist, as will become apparent later on, but they do want to rescue their country from the hands of a clique that is no longer capable of governing it. Now, two years on, Modibo Keïta is imprisoned somewhere in the Sahara, and Mali is run by the same lieutenants who carried out the coup. One died afterward, leaving thirteen, which makes Mali the only country in the world to be ruled by thirteen lieutenants. Their photographs are on display everywhere: thirteen extremely serious, black, thirty-year-old faces, thirteen men in green jungle fatigues, who have taken it upon themselves to drag one of the most forlorn countries in Africa out of the mire.

DAKAR IS NOT all that far away, but if you are unlucky with your flight and it is overfull, with stops in Paris, Bordeaux, and Las Palmas, you certainly will not be feeling full of beans by the time you arrive, despite being able to listen, on earphones purchased for £3 and at an altitude of ten kilometers, to a piece for percussion by the Dutch composer Peter Schat. I remembered Dakar airport from other times of year as hot and steamy, but now there was even a cool sea breeze blowing. The entrance hall was chaotic. African airports call for a degree of serenity fit for the Vatican—it is perfectly useless getting worked up, and at the end of it all you emerge outside anyway, and it turns out that everyone still loves you.

Still groggy from the flight you stand in a high-walled yellow room, surrounded by an eager multitude that wants to change money, carry cases, provide lodgings, and then a stricter cordon that scrutinizes passports and poses questions. And finally the door to Africa opens, and I drive along the coast to my hotel, fifteen kilometers outside Dakar. It is well known here in Africa and, like all the other hotels in Dakar, invariably full. Now too. But the reservation was made more than a month ago? Oh no. Oh yes, look, here is the form. Ah yes, the form, ha ha! But there is nothing in my book! Very beautiful, long black hands rummage through the pages but cannot find me. Someone is phoned, spoken to, then screamed at. Outside the palms rustle, behind them the sea, and I would quite like to go to bed. An hour later I am allowed to. In a genuine hut, twenty meters from an ocean thundering like a jet fighter taking off. A hotel employee, in a pair of vast white knicker-bockers, race-walks ahead of me on white mules along the dark path. The air is salty and damp, a frog croaks somewhere, every-thing smells heavy and spicy, and I really feel I am in Africa. There are so many stars that even the lights on the fishing boats seem to be included; stars floating on the water. I experience a moment of cosmic pride, undergo a metaphysical relationship with the over-whelming firmament, tempered by clichéd notions like "only this morning I was in Amsterdam and now I'm in ... et cetera," and fall asleep, a twentieth-century supermarket-Stanley in a hut with a shower.

The following morning reveals archaic scenes. Sprinklers keep the grass strewn with pearls and thus soft for white feet, a beau-tiful black woman passes by with a fractious white infant bound to her hip, an extremely tall black man exercises an obviously white dog; everything is as it should be. Later on, when I describe this to someone whose social insights are founded more on statistics than on sentiment, he shrugs and says: "What do you expect? Every hotel has its employees. In Spain they're white, in Africa they're black."

That morning at the IFAN (Institut Fondamental de l'Afrique Noire) I try to find a particular professor who can provide me with introductions, but he is not around. "This afternoon perhaps."

The town is crowded and bustling. Much yelling and sounding of claxons in the cheerful morning light, a market full of fish and colors, and then all of a sudden a new friend. He comes toward me beaming, in his neat European clothes and cries "Aha! Bernard!," shakes my hand, slaps me on the shoulder, and simply cannot believe that I am not Bernard. You're not? But surely you're staying in the Hotel N'Gor? Yes, that's true. Well then, surely we spoke to one another yesterday? No. But he has already taken me by the arm and is propelling me across the market. Yes, he is a student. Of course, Senghor *is* a great man, but the students are still going on strike when Pompidou comes. The president is far too chummy with the French. Meanwhile, with imperious gestures, he shoos away sundry young boys who are attempting to sell me things, points to an imitation-antique instrument, a type of gamelan, with narrow planks of wood, each producing a different tone, and tells me this is where the Europeans got their idea for the piano from. He keeps referring to me affectionately as Bernard, his dancing gait and cheery glance in tune with the rest of the sunny scene—that is until we arrive at a café where he thinks I ought to have coffee, and calculates that so far we have done about £1.50's worth of walking. My old-colonial Dutch mercantile spirit manages to beat him down to two francs in local currency, whereupon he departs, rancorously, in search of the next Bernard.

I walk around for a bit, buy some poems by the recently deceased David Diop: "Listen to the scream of a hundred peoples as they break their bonds / listen to my blood of so many years of exile / blood destined to dry up in a coffin of words / find again the fire that breaks through the mist / listen comrades of the centuries-old inferno / from Africa to the Americas—harken to the black summons / it signifies the dawn / the sign of brother-hood that will succour the dreams of the people."

And some by Léopold Senghor: "Totem / I must bury him deep in my veins / the forefather with his skin of storm shot through with thunder and sheet lightning / my animal-guard, I must hide him so that I do not burst through the wall of outrage / he is my true blood who demands loyalty / and protects my naked pride / from the scorn of more fortunate races."

Half an hour later I am sitting among different totems; the Gitane totem, the Rafaél Quinquina totem, the Pernod totem, the white bodies in bikinis totem, the lobster totem, and the oyster totem, all gathered on a terrace-style enclave built on poles, high above the ocean. In the distance, on an idyllic hill, the poet-president's palace shimmers, the sun shines pitilessly down, black bodies lie on the beach, I crack open a shrimp and read in *Le soleil* that a young man has thrown himself from a fourth-floor balcony on the avenue Lamine Guéye, that the Chinese are strengthening their army, that world champion catch-wrestler Power Mike is coming to fight in Demba Diop Stadium, and that Guinea's ambassador has been ordered forthwith to leave Dakar.

Anyone still out of doors moves more slowly now. Later that afternoon I return to the IFAN and manage to find the man I am looking for. And for the first time I run into that strange web of mistrust that I will subsequently come across so often in Mali. Introductions? Information? But who sent you? Only when it transpires that I have read an article by him in *Présence Africaine*, and that one of Chaban-Delmas's secretaries has mentioned his name to me, do we drive together to a pavement café on the seafront. I see from my notebook that a woman sporting a towering silver headdress walked past our table, a brown vulture glided above the beach, just as the gulls do at home, and that there was a garishly mauve piece of material draped over two pieces of black rock, but all I really remember is the end of our conversation when, on reaching his car, he turned to me saying, "*Soyez discret*," and, having got in, added through the window, "And don't mention my name." "But Holland, it's so far away, and who's going to read it?" "Yes, but even so." By then he has provided me with a list of names—ministers, lieutenants, writers—but predicted that no one will be prepared to talk. "My country is at a transitional stage. Everyone watches everyone. Everyone knows everyone. In countries like ours there's only a small elite. We're all family." He tells me that the African intellectual has a far more prominent position, compared to Europe. "The African peoples have a great admiration for, and trust in, an education which they themselves have not enjoyed." He is Muslim, "as you are Catholic maybe," but tells me that, despite centuries of Islam, just below the surface animism is still very influential. "You mustn't forget that animism, unlike Islam, does not recognize sin as such. To us it's a rather foreign concept." Although he admires Léopold Senghor, the president of Senegal, he considers him "a white Negro," and dismisses the novel by fellow countryman Ouologuem, *The Right to Violence*, a ferocious personal mythology based on the situation in Mali, which has been translated throughout the world, as "a European book." "The eroticism it portrays is a lie. It is European eroticism. As far as the African male is concerned Woman does not exist. So that puts paid to all your notions of eroticism, doesn't it?"

Another cosmic night in my hut, and then off to the airport, where all hell has broken loose. In front of the Air Afrique desk the gladiators have joined battle. Everybody wants to be checked in first, and therefore it all takes much longer. It is a veritable witches' cauldron, people pushing and shoving; rich Senegalese get porters to push and shove on their behalf, the hour of departure is fast approaching, and poor old pale-face from Holland is getting exactly nowhere. Mild panic. But seeing as there is only one flight a week to Bamako there is nothing for it but to gird my loins and push with the best of them. Half an hour later I emerge from the sweating, shoving, shouting mass complete with ticket. A corpulent black American approaches me: "Would you mind explaining to this guy that I don't require him to check in my suitcase? He wants money and I don't have any more of their fucking money." The porter, still sweating from the effort of getting past me, stands there like a supplicant in his long brown *boubou*, lisping "dollar, dollar" at intervals, which probably is not quite what the poets of the *négritude* movement had in mind. The fact is that many Africans have a marked dislike of American blacks, a case of mutually distorted vision. Any American, black or otherwise, who can afford to go on a package tour to Africa has to put up with what is to them inconceivable lack of comfort outside the large towns. The black members of such a group, torn between the dream of returning to their roots and a barely suppressed, middle-class feeling of superiority toward those they regard as the "primitive" members of their race, frequently come across as arrogant to Africans. In the company of white men, and not speaking French, they find it difficult to let themselves be waited upon by black men, but get impatient, American style, if things take too long. Burdened with my own so different complexes, I strap myself into the very last seat on the Caravel, and catch myself wondering whether the pilot who will fly us is black or white. What is this, then? Flight neurosis or a knee-jerk racist fear? But black is the color of the pilot, and after a few hours' flight over an utterly barren and stony landscape, we land in Bamako. Definitely a creature of another stripe. In the first place, hot. The ground dry and dusty. And the eerie quiet of an airport with only one plane on the tarmac. You look back and there it is, that contraption in which you have just flown, a prehistoric colossus with a few figures beneath it. Most of the passengers are flying on to Ouagadougou, the capital of Upper Volta.

A small, stocky man with a Lumumba-style goatee beard has already latched onto me. It is an art form. Not everyone can do it. It happens in South America, Spain, Morocco, and the whole of Africa. Someone who attaches himself to you, who adopts you. He looks fearfully grumpy, does not utter a word, and becomes a great friend. I had expected some stern interrogation in what is, after all, a country ruled by a totalitarian regime, but the expression on the official portrait of Lieutenant Moussa Traoré is more melancholic than stern, and the entire form-filling and health ceremony passes off in an atmosphere of gentle resignation. Ten minutes later we are sitting in a old green-and-gray Peugeot. Yesterday, I was in a country I called Africa too. But that had something seductive about it, an easy, pleasing quality. Here, things get serious. It is immense, a poignant, massive, futile endlessness—parched and deserted. A landscape simultaneously exuding unimaginable power and a matchless melancholy. A moonscape, but with people added. That is quite enough of that, I reflect, as I think these thoughts, but like all extreme landscapes this one nestles inside me, never to depart.

At the hotel the chauffeur hands me his card. Yanussa Sagou, chauffeur, transporter, Oulofbougou, rue 106 X 137, Bamako, République du Mali. There is no getting away from it any more.

Walking is becoming arduous. He will come back this afternoon at three. The hotel is too good to be true. A tarnished, colonial pile in a street full of amazingly tall trees. The entrance hall is a sort of atrium where all manner of things are happening. Waiters in long green knickerbockers move around smiling vaguely, the black woman in traditional dress at the reception desk is once again far too pretty, and reclining in the easy chairs are the sort of people who are always thrown together in second-rate films, when yet another international airliner is stranded in a remote desert. They vary from vague, mafia types who deal in masks to VSO volunteers up from the bush for a day in town, guffawing, garrulous black guys who have just bunged a new layer of freshly prepared masks into the ground with a dash of hydrochloric acid, in preparation for next year's export, a member of a Finnish trade delegation, three antediluvian Australian ladies and a lieutenant in khaki with his sleeves rolled up, a stern-looking member of the new elite. *Le beau monde!* My room is a high-ceilinged, gray place. On the wall there is a German poster advertising "*Adel Verpflichtet*" (Noblesse Oblige), an enormous propeller hangs from the ceiling, and a rough-hewn hole in the outside wall houses an air conditioner that starts up with a deafening explosion and makes so much noise that I keep it turned off. There is a rock-hard straw mattress on the bed, and apart from this just the memories of sultry nights spent by long-deceased colonials.

I buy a map, manage to escape Yanussa's eagle eye, and walk to where I think the market is, past the railway track that comes from Dakar and has ground to a halt here in Bamako, past the Leprosy Institute, past an ashen man left for dead in the dust of the roadside. It is starting to get hot. And then it happens. There is no other way to describe it: at the market, I trip over time and am sent flying into a different economy, a different way of behaving. I

plummet out of my world but not into theirs, reduced to a terrible sort of outcast, a true alien. The first thing that comes into my head is that it has an Old Testament quality about it, whatever that means. I probably simply mean "ancient," in the antiquated sense, something that should have disappeared ages ago. There is nowhere else, no other country where I have experienced this sensation so strongly, there are always get-out clauses, references. Not here. A crowd of thousands, stretching over kilometers, milling around happily, all manner of races and dress, everyone utterly absorbed in something, groups of men in turbans and baggy robes, bleating sheep, patriarchs, women with children on their backs, dried fish, millet, cane, strange stones, muddy-colored sauces, fruit, hearts, tripe, herbs. My head is spinning, literally, but I cannot stop, I walk further and further into the market. Nobody pesters you with things you do not want, as they do in Dakar, and if it were not for the fact that occasionally someone smiles at me I would have assumed I was invisible. Now I understand the French expression "un bain de foule." I am letting this crowd wash over me, submerging myself in a way of life whose last shadows disappeared from my world centuries ago—I am already feeling nostalgic even though I am still here. I have never seen so many beautiful people in my life: the women move like Balinese dancers, nobody is wearing Western clothes, the colors swirl, sparkle, and shimmer. I drink a Stork (*"la bière adaptée au climat"*) at a stall, and it occurs to me that I ought to buy a hat—my poor white head is not designed for this—but the only one I can find is a heavy Vietnamese hat of woven twigs, ending in a point, the type always worn by panto Chinamen in revue sketches. Improbably disguised in this fashion, 006 wanders back to the Grand Hotel and takes his daily antimalaria quinine pill.

Days of method and madness ensue. Various scripts, all jumbled up together. The first scenario is that of the journalist who wanted too much, who sought to understand the intricacies of the endless variety of ethnic groups and their history, who bought a number of studies in Paris about the fabulous, mythical empires that existed in Mali during our Middle Ages, from which scarcely anything tangible remains, though there is a good deal of oral tradition. But he is stymied once here by a glut of self-imposed specialist documentation and a dearth of visible historical corroboration. Among the twenty-three different ethnic groups the most important are the Bambaras, the Peulh, the Senoufos, the Tuareg, the Moren, the Sarakollé, the Songhai, and the Malinke. They are divided into hierarchical casts. They identify one another's ancestry by their names, and even now, in the present century, can tell whether they come from a family of warriors, aristocrats, singers, smiths, liberated slaves, or merchants. These are all nuances that escape the casual visitor and I wonder which is worse: simply not knowing, or the nagging awareness that a crucial part of a society completely eludes you.

This is an awkward bone of contention for young African intellectuals. On the one hand, proud of their history, with its diversity, internal rivalries, and age-old traditions, they wish to preserve it all, to rebel against the mandatory British history that is so much less real to them, and is at best an equally voracious and tribalistic conflict of interests, which only has to be mastered because Europe still calls some of the shots. On the other hand, insomuch as it is still the daily reality, it is precisely this aspect of their history that must be done away with: for how can you get a modern state off the ground when it is liable to founder immediately on antiquated enmities and traumas? As the Republic of Mali's government publication puts it: "In order to unify and democratise the country's customs and practices and to adapt the social structures to modern evolution, a recent government decree has put an end to the distinctions between races and castes within the confines of the country." It is probably not quite that simple. Walking along the street or at the marketplace with Yanussa, he will unerringly point out who comes from where, be it recently or in the more distant past, and flipping through the telephone directory with a local writer what emerges is nothing but caste and race. True, it is presented anecdotally, as a thing of the past and pretty inconsequential, but when we get to his own name, he points out that it (Diabété) means "bard" and is essentially what indicates his social standing to everyone, and that all "bards" must defend one another unto death, though of course this does not still apply, but nevertheless, and so on. The Ntu editorial (ntu is Bantu and means "human," or "humanity") states it more baldly: "We want to put an end to the European method that

seeks to classify Africans as Negroid, Bantu, Nilotic, Charmitic...
differentials which to us are meaningless because they are not
based on an in-depth analysis of African philosophy. Their impe-
rialist classification is of no interest to us, what matters is our
common attitude toward life, culture and tradition ..."

Meanwhile, the African and European treasure hunters
calmly carry on delving. Anyone realizing just what an incredible amount of diverse historical, ethnological, and sociological
studies the Africa Institute in Leiden contains cannot but be
staggered, and in my case the staggering culminates in a sheer
knock-out of admiration when I consider just how many years
of work each of these studies takes. Each narrow specialization
often entails total identification with the subject, which in turn
necessitates endless patient field research, frequently in the most
primitive conditions, peeling away the layers, delving into that
immeasurable treasure trove of language, philosophy, and tradition called Africa. Just to take a few of the subjects covered in
two randomly chosen numbers of the *Cahiers d'études Africaines*,
published by Mouton in The Hague: "Psychosis and social
change in the Tallensi of northern Ghana; The North African
state of Tahert and its relations with western Sudan at the close
of the eighth century and in the ninth century; Uniformity
and dualism in the concept of "evil" among the eastern Bantus;
The feudal character of the political system of the Mossi;
Report on the ethno-linguistic mission in the Cameroon;
Psychopathological study of the migrations in Senegal." In other
words, you can spend money like water and read yourself silly,
but for an outsider like me it all boils down to the same thing:
now that I am here, walking around, taking it all in, I have
the same feeling I had as a child when I walked across the ice
of the newly frozen lakes at Loosdrecht for the first time, of a

mysterious world just below my feet, full of everything, plants, animals, secrets, indefinably but very powerfully present.

The second scenario is far more absurd. Anyone wanting to take photographs in Mali has to have permission. And anyone wanting to do it in a professional capacity needs more permission still. The photographer who has come to join me does not have any, and going ahead without it is risky, because the starting point is usually arrest and according to insiders it is a hell of a job getting the offender out of jail once inside. Armed with all manner of wonderful instructions we venture forth on a merry-go-round of officialdom. But it is no good. Day after day we come up against a wall of polite bureaucracy and crazy stipulations, getting lost in a maze of boiling hot waiting rooms. The regulation, as a whole string of polished gentlemen explain to us from behind their desks, has been inherited from the former regime, when all freedoms were severely curtailed. But surely that regime has been gone these past two years? Ah yes, but the regulation still applies. Everyone agrees that it is ridiculous, and in direct conflict with all those government statements about encouraging tourism. We ascend to ever greater heights, smoking Dunhills with diminutive German-speaking black men in European dress, and Sobranies with tall French-speaking black men in ornately embroidered *boubous*, gaining a lot of friends along the way, but not the piece of paper. After hours, accompanied by a whiskey in the dusty bar of the Grand Hotel, they explain: no one wants to grant permission on anyone else's behalf, everyone is on their guard, they all have to cover their backs—"this bureaucracy is a curse, it's the reason nothing's possible and nothing gets done"—then the stories start: about the Italian journalist who had written something unflattering and the Common Market journalists who had not been very complimentary either. I do not even remember how it all got solved, just that one day some body returned from somewhere abroad and added his precious signature, so that now at least a start can be made on the third scenario, Yanussa's. He regards all the fuss about the permit as a lot of nonsense. If we had let him organize it, he says, things would have been resolved long ago. Nor can he muster any enthusiasm for a visit to a far-flung nature reserve. He's taken *toubabs* (white men) there so often; they spend the whole day waiting for an elephant to pass by, and when it does not they get sore. Why don't we go to the zoo? So that is where we go, to the zoo, situated between the town and the presidential hill. En route, beyond the last old-colonial villas, brightly colored billboards boast flights to Budapest, East Berlin, and Moscow, a gentle reminder for the president, who passes this way each day in a high-speed limo, flanked by the traditional escort of serious-looking outriders. Because it is such a small town I have already glimpsed him a few times, a tall, athletic man with sad eyes. Along with three Tuareg we are the sole visitors to the zoo, a collection of neglected cages with few animals. Yanussa is not very keen on the Tuareg, and they do indeed appear huge: tall and lean with gaunt imperious faces beneath their turbans. They come to town to sell tooled leather products and buy weapons, and they have taken the afternoon off to do a spot of animal baiting. "Bloody racists," Yanussa says, "they're extremely vicious and they never miss." And so we trudge on, carting the heat with us like a backpack, past Mali the hippo, Sulawula the red monkey, Srugu the spotted hyena, and Bakorongourou the wild cat. There is something sad about them, these animals—at home yet still incarcerated, they sit in the tough dry grass that pushes up inside the cages as well, leaning against the rusty bars, looking miserable and slightly malevolent. I want to know the names of trees, and point and inquire. "A French tree," Yanussa says. And that one? "A French tree also." Clearly we will not pass muster as naturalists.

Then it is time to drive back to town, to the small mosque in his neighborhood, where prayers will be starting at about seven. He parks his car in front of the building so that we are able to observe how a small Peugeot van returns every few minutes to drop off yet more old men. It is the owner of a cinema, a pious man, who volunteers to pick up the elderly each day. Some of them go inside, others proceed to sit down outside in the sand; swathed in their baggy clothes they acknowledge one another with slow gestures, then a tall thin man in a bright blue djellaba appears and at once starts chanting. The sky has turned the color of ash, the voice pierces the evening unremittingly, the old men sidle across the sand toward the mosque in crab-like fashion; through the entrance I watch them bowing down and praying. I wonder whether we are in the way, but Yanussa says, "Even if a snake comes and sits in front of him a true Muslim will not look up during prayers." Fair enough. "And why do some of them remain outside in the sand praying?" "Because they're not wearing the correct attire."

As we are driving off, all at once he says: "In Moscow, Khrushchev told some of our students that heaven doesn't exist." I ask him what he thinks of this, but he only shrugs his shoulders and remarks cryptically: "We black people are easily deceived." I ask him how he views the Chinese, of whom there are many in these parts. He replies by driving us past the firmly locked gate of the Chinese Embassy; it is garishly painted, a gate straight out of an opera set. There is no one about. "We find the Chinese ugly," he says, "so that children call one another Chinese at school, as a term of abuse. But they are hard workers. In Mopti they built a hotel in six weeks. And after six in the evening they're nowhere to be seen. They always stick together. We respect them. They do a lot for us. So do the Fathers. But not the Russians. The Russians exploit us. They look down on us."

"And the others?" "*Les autres? C'est bon. C'est le tourisme, c'est le commerce.* Before, under Modibo, things were bad. No commerce, no tourists, no work." And pointing his straight African finger right between my eyes he adds: "*Et pas de travail, pas d'argent.*" And no money, no women, or rather no money, no marriage. For sleeping together is okay, but you will not persuade a woman to leave the family home, nor will you be permitted to move in with her, before you have first paid a dowry in exchange. I ask him whether he is married. No, he is divorced. And when she left he had to pay up yet again. Now he lives with his family. He's got no money for a new wife. "Oh, I could take a country girl, but you know what it's like, you bring them to town, you teach them how to behave in a civilized manner, and then along comes some big, good-looking guy and they're off." I can tell by his voice that this has probably happened to him. Is he alone now? No, he does have a girlfriend. What will they do if she gets pregnant? Or does she take the pill? The pill? No, that's not for us. Why not? It just isn't. *Ce n'est pas pour les noirs.* Period. He wants me to see the final moments of the sunset above the Niger, drives out of town, over the big bridge, parks the car, and together we walk through the sand along the river bank. The big wheel of the sun is sinking into the empty plain, the river is low and silent, and we make our way to the upturned hull of a boat and sit down among the prattling guinea fowl. A bit further along fishermen are mending nets, three women—their Ethiopian-dancer's bodies silhouetted against the sunlight—are washing themselves in the ever darkening water, young boys work on a boat and talk quietly in Malinke, a loosely robed man kneels with his back to the last rays of sun and says his prayers next to the reeds, a flock of dark-colored birds passes by and disappears into the plain, itself dissolving into mist.

We head back to town. The whole place is imbued with a sweet, heavy peace. In the sandy main square surrounding the mosque, men squat by fires and torches, wrapped in their cloaks, eating. I ask who they are and Yanussa says: "They don't have any family to eat with." The circles are large, the men mostly young, there is music and the sound of quiet singing; they are eating chunks of roasted meat or orange-colored rice from bowls. "They come in from the bush to work here in town." So where do they sleep? "Anywhere." It is the same at the station. People are sitting and lying in the hall and on the platforms. An old Negro squats, shitting, with his face to the wall. The train does not go any further into Africa beyond here, it is the end of the line, there is no train today and maybe there will not be another one, ever. The clock is broken, has stopped at an impossible hour. I buy a packet of Liberté and return to my hotel.

The dining room is almost deserted; there is better food to be had elsewhere. While chewing on my *capitaine*, a large fresh-water fish, I am caught unawares by a becalmed sort of melancholy. It does not get much uglier than this. The ceiling is gray and has bush huts in an unreal gloomy night painted on it, as if a neon moon is shining over an ashen earth. The curtains used to be yellow, the orange tablecloth is faded, hanging from the grimy walls is the odd dusty mask, there are redundant water coolers on every table, two chandeliers in which almost none of the lamps work and those that do are of varying wattage, the chairs are green, and next to me an extremely orange lamp spotlights the wall. Somewhere behind a partition I hear a masticating voice announce that, "at the embassy they take American money," and the unbridled evening rolls on.

A few hours later I have an appointment with a young writer. I am met by aggressive dogs, who only quiet down after some minutes. He has already made it abundantly clear over the telephone that he will not talk about politics, absolutely not. When I arrive he is not there. His white wife talks scathingly about the rest of the French community. "They still think it's fifteen years ago." We are drinking whiskey and sitting in the half-darkness of the veranda, amid the rustlings and stirrings of the increasingly chilly evening. I tell her I bought several of her husband's books in Paris, his transcriptions of traditional Malinese tales, but that their meanings often escape me. He arrives an hour later, a tall, gently swaying figure with a hesitant expression. What do I want? If it is about politics he has nothing to say, and if I do find anyone, besides official government spokesmen, willing to speak, then they're bound to be people who run no risk and are therefore "of no consequence."

Only later do I manage to elicit from him that he has recently been fired from an important government function, and the following morning I hear that a large number of trade union leaders have been arrested during the night. He tries to give me some idea of the labyrinthine mosaic of castes and slaves, all with their own rites and regulations. Of course there are no slaves any more, but you can tell by a name from which of the four types of slave someone is descended. Just as you can tell from his name, Diabété, that he's a Nyamakala—not a Noumou (a smith) or Loebé (a wood turner), but a Dialé—a bard, singer, poet, writer. They come next after the aristocracy, which is itself subdivided into three main castes. In short, a circuit of signs and meanings by which the English class system pales in comparison, more elaborate than the *Almanach de Gotha* or a catalogue of club ties. He is fascinated by his country's oral tradition, and spends his free time making excursions into the bush to record the old folktales—as a Dialé he has access to all the other Dialés, and there are still plenty of old men who know the songs, some of them dating back to the twelfth and thirteenth centuries. He puts on a tape. A stringed instrument plays in monotonous but ever-shifting circles. An

elderly male voice joins in, singing about the epos of the mythical
Emperor Sun Jata. We listen in silence, but oh how differently!
All I hear is the music, apart from that I have been struck stone
deaf, I am like a Papuan at one of Alban Berg's operas, a hopeless stupidity has taken hold of me, it is all completely lost on me,
each word, each sound means something, and then something
else again, but I am just someone sitting on a patio, hearing tones.
Quietly he begins to translate: "*A di benye labo a kala do*—he takes
the arrows out of their quiver | *K'a la birilan basilan lu kima*—he
covers himself in clothes full of fetishes | *K'a n'i lo wéré da la*—he
has gone into the bush | *K'a dun were kono ware nofè*—he is moving
toward the lion | *K'a bun bényé la wara ba*—he has loosed an arrow
at the lion . . ." but there is more and more he wants to tell me,
explain to me, write down for me, and the more I understand, the
more I realize just how much I do not understand, until eventually we give up and just go on listening to that voice in the lisping
night. A voice that, two or three generations on, will no longer
mean anything, will be truly antiquated, a canned myth sitting
on a shelf in a UNESCO-funded museum, an African memento
of glory days, cherished heroes, history, until MacLuhan's village
scores the ultimate equalizer and anything, anywhere, that was
"of the people" becomes an expensive plaything for an unhearing
posterity. We say our sentimental farewells, and I take potluck,
walking along dark avenues into what I hope is the town, which
itself consists of little more than avenues anyway, a tropical
Dulwich Village, with a few dilapidated government buildings,
the odd hotel, side avenues with embassies tucked away in crumbling colonial houses, and one high school with a truck full of
armed soldiers in front of it. I hail a taxi and ask whether I can
see some dancing somewhere. Yes, pupils trying for a place with
the National Ballet practice behind the main mosque. As I walk
through the gate toward the courtyard I hear the sound of drums.

The only spectators are two boys. A single bulb hangs from a long cord trailing from a darkened building. In that dim light I catch sight of the dancers. I do not know how long I sat there, concealed by the night, unnoticed by anyone. The rhythms grew wilder and wilder, the dancers, boys and girls, smote the ground with their bare feet, as if they wanted to kick the earth aside; I remember a panting menace, a kind of tremendous animal energy, as though they all formed one livid, stamping, sweating body, more and more aroused, spreading and shrinking, then two belligerent snakes, then a black, somber, impenetrable block, not the abstraction of a ballet, but sheer dancing existence, nothing left but dance, each movement stretching the body further and more rapidly than I have ever seen. It is like a powerful slap in the face, and at the same time it is a—God, what a word!—sublime exercise in nostalgia, but for what, lest it be for a distant, long-lost ability to be at one with one's own body, or, that that body should just once express what one is, without reserve or frustration? After an hour I extricate myself. Me, someone who knows how to make a *lyonnaise* sauce and where to eat the best fish when you are in London, who would rather hear Bach's cello suites played by Rostropovich than by Starker, who values Vestdijk's[*] earlier novels above his later ones, has been to Venice twice, prefers the *NRC* to *Het Parool*[†], and who now suddenly feels like affluence's deprived lackey. As a punishment I go on to dream about the dancing all night long in my stuffy bedroom, and it is not pleasant. The market, the zoo, the soldiers, the dancers, all crowd into my dreams, I wake up confused and walk over to the balcony and see, beneath the softly waving tamarind trees in the deathly silent street, the open trucks full of soldiers passing by.

[*] Simon Vestdijk (1898–1971), prolific Dutch author of thirty-eight novels and more than twenty volumes of poetry.

[†] NRC and *Het Parool*, Dutch Newspapers.

The following morning Bernard d'Arras, director of the UTA, a tall aristocratic Frenchman, twenty years in Africa, never wants to leave, comes to collect me. I ask him whether he found the changeover from colonial to ordinary white resident difficult, but he has taken it all in his stride. You have to be able to adapt, he says, and illustrates this capacity perfectly by plotting a course worthy of a Venetian courtier through the small groups of Sten gun–toting soldiers guarding the Ministry of Home Affairs. Our goal: Lieutenant Filifing Cissoko, member of the CMLN, the Military Committee of National Liberation, one of the thirteen who toppled Modibo Keïta and who now rule the country. We know the committee is due to meet at nine o'clock, have worked out at what time the lieutenant will therefore need to leave his ministry, and we have timed it all so well that suddenly, on a rickety wooden landing, we find ourselves standing face to face with a steely-eyed giant in paramilitary uniform. We are blocking his way and he is not happy about it. D'Arras, who is the same height, improvises something halfway between a bow and a military salute, punctuated with copious "*mon lieutenants*" but "*mon lieutenant*" casts a cool eye over us and departs with sirens wailing, abandoning us to the care of his adjutant, who gives us an appointment for the next day. When we meet up again the eye is just as steely, the voice equally abrupt, the interview correct and military. This is a man from the no-nonsense generation. He examines my copy of the Dutch magazine *Avenue*, devoted to Tanzania, and I examine him. On his desk there is a forty-five-centimeter, aluminium-colored statue of V.I. Lenin, and on a ledge at knee height, possibly forgotten by a nervous applicant, a revolutionary manual by Kim Il Sung. No, I cannot see the president. The president's diary is full for the next three months. I am, however, presented with all of his speeches, and by this I do mean *all* of them, including the one marking the inauguration of the Swedish ambassador. The tone: keep foreign relations as open as possible, with as few commitments as is feasible. The phrasing is that of an adroit professional diplomat and has a whiff of an *éminence grise* about it. And as for domestic policy: law and order, reconstruction, one people, one faith, one purpose, the freedom to set one's own priorities, starting with the reorganization of a civil service so weighed down by "laziness, disorder, and indolence" as to be incapable of forming a good basis for a "healthy, dynamic economy." End of interview. He departs for a meeting of the Committee of Thirteen, and I go off to meet an elderly friar from Brabant, in the Netherlands, who has been working in Mali for more than fifty years.

A scraggy little man with a Ho Chi Minh beard, he's extremely on the ball and fluent in Bambara, French, and Dutch, the latter spoken with a perfect Brabantian accent unsullied by the years. I am given a cup of "Dutch coffee"; he can scarcely hear me but that is not really necessary as nothing I have to say could possibly be of interest to him after so long. Mali is his life. He tells me about Bamako "before there was anything there," about the colonial French magistrates who "didn't even notice that the rich used to substitute a poor servant when a family member was to be tried for a crime, because not one of those magistrates had any command of the native language." How he introduced the Malinese to lettuce and pork during the unbelievable 1920s, how he and Weygand's officers went buffalo hunting with cannons, but never shot one—a long and strange life in a country not designed for whites. His nephew, a missionary White Father, comes in with a copy of *Shalom** that has just arrived and places it despondently on the desk. "If only they knew," is his only comment, and before I can question him further on this he is called away to minister to someone who is ill; a tired man, his sandals white with dust. I take

---

* Dutch magazine dedicated to Third World problems and peace.

in the lonely room full of Dutch and English books, and ask myself for the hundredth time what it is that persuades someone to spend a life of poverty and loneliness in a far-flung corner of Africa, in a country where the tangible results will always be minimal. None of which troubles my friar in the least. On his bandaged foot he hobbles with me to the door of the sweltering courtyard and shouts in my ear: "I've lived my whole life in Mali, and I expect I shall die in Mali too. I don't need to go back to Holland again. I hardly know anyone there any more."

THIS IS THE last afternoon in Bamako. Tomorrow we leave for Mopti, and after that Timbuktu. Yanussa drives me along the baking avenues rather aimlessly, but I realize I am no longer taking anything in. My last appointment is with an EEC representative, a small, balding man, sat beneath an enormous map of Mali. "As far as food is concerned the country can support itself," he tells me, "but that's about the extent of it. There are indications that there's oil and bauxite, and the Russians have been digging for gold, but because of Mali's unfortunate, landlocked position extracting it isn't profitable. What the European Development Fund does is attempt to increase the profitability of the existing cultures— cotton, groundnuts, rice—to try to achieve more variety in these cultures and make more land suitable for cultivation." He lists a few of the projects: the war on rinderpest, technological support during the construction of an abattoir, an irrigation project near Lake Télé, and points to small dots all over the immense map, where groups of Europeans are engaged on these projects together with Malinese. He tells me the profits generated go in their entirety to Mali, with nothing flowing back to Europe at all. I ask him what the Chinese are doing. "A lot," he replies shortly. "They're building a brick factory in Mopti. They've taught the Malinese to grow tea. Under their tutelage the army's boots have been made from domestic leather for the first time. They run huge rice projects, live among the population, and don't ask for anything material in return."

Later on someone else puts it more starkly: "A country like Mali resembles a poker chip left lying on the gaming table, only nobody feels like playing at the moment. The country isn't important to the Russians, or to the Americans. It's all on its own, which is why it can use any help it can get. Cattle and fresh-water fish are pretty much the only export earners, it's bound to remain a desperately poor country however efficient the new government is. They're doing their best, but it's a pretty hopeless situation."

When I get back to the hotel there is a note from d'Arras to say that Air Mali has altered its schedules for tomorrow; the plane is leaving five hours earlier, and he will be coming to collect me at 4.45 AM. When I grumble about this to Yanussa he grins maliciously, "*Tu vois? C'est l'Afrique.*"

AND THE FOLLOWING morning I do indeed see. Two hours after departure time the pilot and crew finally appear in the waiting area and proceed to enjoy a light breakfast. The day began with fluttering orange streamers; the Antonov 24, a Russian plane, is parked on the tarmac ready to fly us to Mopti. It's a tight squeeze. Four ancient, or possibly deceased, Americans, Tuareg with alarming weapons in their holsters, women swathed in hundreds of layers of cloth, and a small fat Frenchman working here on a road-building project, who tells me that Air Mali (three aircraft) provides breakfast for its crew because otherwise they would not take any and consequently would not be alert enough. Why do I have this feeling that only now am I really going on a journey? One minute into the flight and the earth is a desolate void once more, and stays that way. At the spot where the air conditioning should be there is just a hole, icy air blasts down my neck, but the stewardess has a sweet round face and sweet round breasts, and wears a hand-woven garment that reaches the ground. A few hours later, after a stopover in Ségou, we arrive in Mopti, where we are met by Herman Haan, who is here on his umpteenth Tellem expedition to Dogon country, and comes in to Mopti on market day to buy provisions. That same afternoon we drive by way of Bandiagara to Sanga, the start of Dogon territory. To begin with, the road is reasonable, but later on the track hurls us at each other in the Land Rover–like rag dolls. The few people we do meet along the way get covered in dry, red dust, but they do not seem to mind. We arrive at the encampment pretty exhausted; it has been a long day since 5 o'clock this morning.

Tables outside on the rocky ground, stone rooms, no electric light, antimosquito screens, all raked together on a biblical plateau. A tall black man with proud, almost oriental, features embraces Haan and welcomes him, and I hear the ritual Dogon greeting for the first time, or rather I hear a series of sounds exchanged, the meaning of which I understand only later: Greetings! Greetings! Are you at peace? Yes, I am. And your wife? She is at peace. And your children? And the whole world? And the animals? But perhaps it is not so much what is said as the fact that people greet one another in this way without fail, on every occasion, as if the fact of meeting is really special, as if talking to one another and hearing about one another are such valuable commodities they have to be cushioned by formulae. I heard it hundreds of times during those few days, until I became envious that I could not do it. *Po? Pol Ia po? Ia po! Oe seoa? Seoa! Umana seoa? Seoa! Pégé seoa? Seoa!* And so on, ad infinitum, but finally ending in a long and satisfied "Aaaaah!"

Herman Haan walks through the village of Ogol with us. It was here, in 1946, that Ogotemmêli the hunter summoned Marcel

Griaule, the French ethnologist who had been doing research in the area since 1931, and in thirty-three successive days proceeded to expound the entire cosmology of the Dogon for his benefit. Thirty-three days that revealed a way of thinking, handed down by word of mouth over the centuries, so complex and astounding that, in Griaule's words, "all the notions about a so-called primitive African mentality were overthrown."

I walk through the village: square dwellings of red mud, topped by strange pointed roofs of straw, like pixie hats. Holy places, sacrificial stones, altars, empty spots you are not allowed to walk through. We pause by the dwelling belonging to the Hogon, or village priest. He is very powerful, the community takes care of him, once chosen he never leaves his courtyard again. Half naked, he sits propped against that wall of dried blood, a wizened, blue-black doll in which only the eyes still move. From behind the wall over which we are leaning Haan greets him in the traditional way. He does not answer, and after a while goes inside. We stand around for a bit, surrounded by a few children who watch us silently with huge eyes. Then he emerges again. He has donned a loose, indigo-colored cloak, and on his ancient mask of a head he wears a brilliant-red headdress, a sort of Phrygian bonnet. The questions and answers fly through the air, and even when we finally take our leave his high-pitched old man's voice still follows us.

Evening is approaching. Haan leaves for his bivouac among the rocks an hour away, where the other members of the Tellem expedition are waiting for him, and we arrange for his guide Diankulo to collect us the following morning at six, for a trip to the rock face. That night, by the light of a flickering oil lamp, I read about the god Amma, who created the earth in the likeness of a woman's body, with an anthill for her genitalia and a termite hill for her clitoris. After he has created her he wants to sleep with her, but then for the first time something goes wrong in the universe, the termite hill rises up, exhibiting its manliness; the clitoris is a phallus, the copulation cannot take place. But God is almighty. He plucks out the termite hill and possesses the circumcised earth. And the jackal is born, symbol of God's tribulations. A second coming together achieves a better result. The earth = woman is now circumcised, the clitoris = penis has been removed, the water = holy seed penetrates deep into the earth, a pair of twins are born, the Nommo, ever-present in the art of the Dogon. Their bodies are green and supple, their arms without joints, the top half of them is human, the lower half snake, and their skin glistens like the surface of water. They are a perfectly formed double, which has eight limbs. That is why its (their) number is eight, the figure that represents the world. Because it is made from his seed the Nommo contains God's essence, namely: the support, shape, and raw material of the life force, source of mobility, and endurance. And this force is Water. The twins *are* every drop of water, *of* every drop of water, *in* every drop of water. Later that night I fall asleep in the knowledge that next day I will be moving through a world about which I have only the vaguest, most paltry of notions.

It is precisely 6 AM when Diankulo knocks on my door. The light outside is gray. Ten minutes later we are on our way across the high rocky plateau. It is cold. There are baobabs dotted around, monkey-bread trees, and behind me in the village I can hear the dull, rhythmic thudding of women mashing millet. Sheep bleat, cockerels crow. Diankulo keeps up a brisk pace, and I walk behind without speaking. Half an hour later there is no sound except the wind, and a distant chuckling that he says must be monkeys. At the bivouac they are all up, about six of them—anthropologists, biologists, students—here to search for the enigmatic Tellem people who disappeared without trace, leaving their mysterious mud towers, taciturn idols, and thousands upon thousands of skeletons behind them, among these steep, inaccessible, rocky escarpments. We clamber over to the rock in which the expedition is spending three months. High up on the escarpment their "soft machine" is attached by means of a pulley, which allows them to winch themselves to a burial cave higher up, full of thousands of skeletons to be selected and measured. Why, a few of them are even destined to travel to the Netherlands, oh wondrous scholarship.

An hour later we enter the valley. There are five of us now, Herman Haan in the lead like a Roman centurion, with us following in formation; it is a day's hike along narrow footpaths, the world comes to an end beyond Sanga and cars cannot reach here. As we descend deeper the bushes and trees get greener, occasionally I hear the bubbling of a spring and Diankulo tells me that is where monkeys and other wild animals go to drink in the early morning. I see a black butterfly, like a floating, cheerful angel of death, birds as tiny as my little finger, invisible turtle doves clap their wings and their sweet calls rebound off the valley walls. For a long time we meet no one, and then suddenly we come across an old man in a white robe, leaning on a splendidly elaborate staff. As we pass one another the greeting begins, and it continues even when he has rounded a bend in the path and disappeared from sight. This litany can be endlessly prolonged, and I consider all the things I did not get the chance to ask him: "And the clouds?" They are at peace! "And the trees?" They are at peace! "And the cosmos?" It is at peace! Hours later we reach the village. It clings to the steep rock face like a burr, the landscape around us is etched with an almost bathetic precision—outcrops of orange rock, ivy, white flowers, trees with tiny, silver-sharp leaves—and deep down below our feet, a pale, dusty plain that fades away into the horizon. We are received by the village elders in the "conversation house," a low, open space, topped by an extremely thick roof of dried rushes and bunches of twigs, resting on four tree stumps rubbed smooth and shiny by the years.

Below me a man sits pleating a mat, someone else is weaving a snow-white length of cloth, and apart from the sounds of a few animals, and Diankulo's soothing powwow with the village elders, all is quiet. A silent eagle hangs motionless, directly above us. Haan points out that some of the dwellings have the shape of a mother's body. I ask him how, despite the dry heat, the savannah in the distance can be so vague, and he says it is red sand from a distant Sahara storm. Only now do I notice how insolently erect the burnished escarpment stands in the surrounding landscape. I see that its lofty summit is covered in the strange towers of the Tellem, and I wonder how on earth they managed to get up there.

THE BURIAL CAVES of the Dogon are situated much lower down. Diankulo informs me that when someone dies the hunters break his bow and put a piece of glowing charcoal in their mouths, as a sign of mourning. Now that is what I call grieving! As soon as someone dies, their body is washed with water fresh from the well. Their hair is shorn. They are wrapped in a cotton winding cloth, the feet remaining bare. The corpse is laid out on the "stone of the brave," upon a bier of branches. The living give thanks to the one who has died: "Thank you for the millet / Thank you for the animals / Thank you for yesterday / Thank you for the good deeds." After this the deceased is taken to the burial cave, but the men run back to his dwelling and burst inside, firing their rifles, staging mock fights, while the women wail laments and beat empty calabashes, (empty, for the dead have no more need of drink). This goes on for days. Only much later does the Dama commence, a ceremony designed to accompany the soul of the deceased, which is still roaming the village, to its forefathers. On this journey his soul, or *nyama*, is the equal of the *nyamas* of all the people or animals killed by him during his lifetime, and is therefore vulnerable to their revenge. A voice from another world—that of the bull-roarer—announces the beginning of this ceremony. A thin wooden or metal plaque with notched edges is spun in the air by an initiate, producing a moaning sound. The women and children must then keep out of sight. By the light of the moon, until dawn, the bull-roarer player follows a traditional route close to the deserted village. For the Dogon the bull-roarer is the voice of the first ancestor to encounter death; its tone also recalls the revelation of speech to mankind. Masked dances are held on the roof of the burial cave—masks with wings, masks depicting the ancestors, lion masks, horseman masks—they all help the deceased on his way, a final act by a community whose people live together, and consequently do not die alone either.

We say goodbye and continue on, into the considerably hotter afternoon. The surrounding peace feels like a tangible element, something I could reach out and touch. It is absolutely hushed, not a sound except for our footsteps and our slightly labored breathing, now that we are slowly beginning to climb again. This is a magical valley, a real-life Shangri-La, and sitting at home now, so long afterward, listening to Dogon music, looking at photographs in which people have become what their masks depict, I still get that same feeling of happiness mingled with longing, because it is doubtful that I will ever return. And if I did, would it be the same? How long will our world permit the existence of theirs? The only thing that detracts from the "wholeness" of their society is that it can be seen by us, and it would not be the first time the rot has set in with our looking. Perhaps that is the nostalgia, that it can never stay like this. I discover that I cannot even write about it: if I try to say something about their "community" I flounder around in the most contemptuous neo-Christian terminology, sounding like an acolyte for the more radical wing of the Christian Democrats at election time. We do not have the right to speak about community because we no longer have one in the real sense. It is impossible to apply the same concepts to a society where they have an entirely different import.

We live alone and they live together, or to put it another way, that an old lady can sit dead at her window for three days could not happen there, although there are bound to be those who say that this is because they do not have any windows to sit at.

It is evening by the time we arrive back at the encampment. The last two hours are heavy going. Barely able to climb up the escarpment, we stop to drink every fifteen minutes, and now, despite the size of the bottles of Ivory Coast Flag beer, I just cannot quench my thirst.

ACTUALLY, MALI IS too many countries. After the tropical decors of Bamako, and the lost paradise behind Bandiagara, comes the vision of Mopti—the wide, muddy-colored river with its hundreds of hollowed-out tree trunks, the rowers etched against the pale, broad shoreline behind like hieroglyphs on empty parchment, the miles of marketplace with its orgy of wares and traditional dress; *peulh* women with golden earrings almost bigger than their faces, hajis saying their prayers next to a truck, farmers in black caps sitting far back on their donkeys as though someone else is steering, the imam who whirls into view like an apparition from his cathedral-sized, mud-colored mosque, water-carriers with Vietnamese hats, black hunks of fish, chunks of scaly, glistening salt, yellowish-brown, flyblown cuts of meat, half-naked girls washing themselves by the gondola-like barges, and further up, when I walk along the river, pyramids of red earthenware piled up high, and vultures in a parched field making cruel hacking movements above the half-eaten carcass of a goat. And after all this, the nights in that austere pile, the Chinese Hotel, where an inexorable hush descends after nine at night, and you are left alone with a glaringly white fluorescent light attached horizontally to the wall opposite your bed, the final manifestation of God.

And after this vision, the sand-blown Fata Morgana of Timbuktu. You can see it as you fly over the Sahel—the DC-3 flies low enough. More and more color bleeds from the landscape, even along the river banks there is no longer any green. What we are covering in a few hours' flying would be a journey of some days by Land Rover.

That final week it is like playing in a giant sandpit. Everything is sand and everything has the color of sand. There are no streets, just sandy beaches minus the sea. Independence Square resembles a small desert, and the sentry standing in front of Fort Cheikh Sidi Bekaye, machine gun slung round his neck like a piece of jewelry, is up to his ankles in sand. There is sand in the bread and sand in the rice. There was a time when the whole of Europe and the entire Maghreb trembled with longing whenever they heard the name Timbuktu. During Askia Muhamad Touré's reign, twenty-five thousand students studied here, this was the city of the wise, the intellectual metropolis of western Sudan, but anyone climbing onto the dried-up mud of the mosque rooftop nowadays sees a city made up of little more than huts. Gone are the universities, gone the trade in gold and salt, gone the palace built of stone. The day on which this dream went up in flames is described in one of the oldest chronicles of the Sudan, the Tarikh el Fettach. It is October 20, 1593:

> When all the 'ulamã (learned scribes) had been called together at the mosque by Pasha Mahmoud, the Moroccan fusiliers took up position on all the patios and at all the exits. Hereafter things took place by the will of God, things that are better left unsaid lest the heart be unable to bear it; suffice to say it was the biggest blow ever meted out to Islam as a whole.

MORE THAN SEVENTY 'ulamã were taken off to Morocco in chains, and only Ahmed Baba returned, and according to the chronicle the city became "a body without a soul." The Moroccans—Spanish renegades for the most part—knew what they were about: by destroying the intellectual elite they broke the city, so that the Songhai Empire literally crumbled away. Timbuktu became the faded village it is now, a magnet for the sun's rays; four Land Rovers, eight thousand people, a barracks, a military governor, an encampment for tourists who come looking for something which no longer exists.

The journey's end verges on the Dutch. Seated in a sedan chair and accompanied by a Moorish guide of Orson Wellesian proportions, Countess Frumpheim takes a trip across the river in a pirogue. The land on this side of the river is marshy and, as a result, outlandishly green. Bluish, mysterious water lilies and nenuphars float on the glistening water; white, black, and gray herons crouch

among the reeds on the banks; the two rowers pitch their sticks high into the air and the boat zips forward in perfect silence. The river gets wider and wider, we come to a village with round, bulbous, plaited huts. I see the loveliest woman I have ever seen and vow never to forget her, hundreds of white sheep arrive from the pastures, I no longer know where I am, the Sahara merges into Holland, we row back, the sun grows so big it seems about to engulf the earth, children yell from the banks, *"Toubab, ça va?"* and yes, everything is at peace, I am at peace, the evening is at peace, time itself is at peace, there is even a sort of mist coming up, storks fly past and it is as if they are turning over pages of air, a farmer swims from one bank to the other with his herd, and when we arrive back at the harbor it is dark.

NEXT MORNING we are at the airport by six, but the plane has been delayed by twenty-four hours. It turns out to be a long day. We drive into the desert with our guidebook in search of a caravan we do not manage to find. We come to a watering hole for camels, where oxen on endless chains draw the water from the ground, but the Moorish shepherds are hostile and will not talk to us, the women pull their veils down over their faces. There is no more tea or coffee at the encampment, no beer, no mineral water, and no wine; it was all supposed to arrive with the flight and now it is stuck at Bamako. In my stone cell the frog is still in the shower, the gecko still above the bed, the spiders still frying on the insect screen. The afternoon stretches on; I lie on the bed and think about my journey, about the man in Paris who, before I left, said to me: "Africa? It's never been viable, it's not viable now and it never will be either. I used to be enthusiastic too, but I've been going there for twenty years and it's hopeless. Their entire history consists of bloodshed and murder, and that's how it'll remain." I do not recognize his despair, or his bitterness. Whenever aircraft are twenty-four hours late, all hell breaks loose among European and American passengers. In spoiled isolation, having become asocial through self-indulgence, the white man travels through Africa and sees zilch. And the tourists, who trail in ever-increasing numbers past the odd wild animal and dancing masks for hire, do not see anything either. And yet . . . and yet . . . Lévi-Strauss put it more clearly:

The ethnologists are here to bear witness to the fact that the way we live is not the only way, that there are other ways that have enabled people to live happily. The ethnologists invite us to temper our smugness a little, to respect different patterns of life. The societies studied by ethnologists contain lessons which are worth listening to. They are societies that have managed to achieve a balance between human beings and their natural environment, a balance whose secret and purpose we can no longer fathom.

On the last night we get invited to a Moorish wedding. And me little more than a passer-by! Would anyone in Utrecht invite two blacks, who just happened to be passing, to their wedding? Anyway. The hours pass and my utopian nostalgia fades with the music. I stop thinking about anything. The gold and silver women dance, the same birdlike movements over and over again, the music traces its monotonous rhythms, hours later when we go and sit on the encampment patio for a bit, I can still hear the same drums, beating, beating. The moon is lying on its back in the heavens, there is bound to be a caravan on its way to Timbuktu, a donkey brays, dogs begin to howl, tomorrow someone else will be sitting in this chair, tomorrow it will be hot again. Everything seems as it should be.

1971

When the World Wore a Fool's Cap

"BUT HOW DO I get there?" "If you leave the bay at first light, and sail into the brilliance of the rising sun, following the coastline, you'll soon lose sight of the harbor. That mountain you can see over there, beyond the hills, will not in fact get any closer, so do not let it confuse you. You should keep as close to the coast as possible, making use of the wind, which is usually southerly at this time of year. At a certain point you will arrive at some rocks that resemble a herd of cattle crammed tightly together. From there you go . . ." The first map must have been a map of words.

The second was drawn in sand, or scratched on a rock.

"I do not understand."

"I'll draw it for you."

OF COURSE IT did not happen like that; or perhaps it did. A jagged line, carved in the damp sand with a stick, and words that accompanied the drawing: words that stood for cliffs, stars, reefs, places to drop anchor, currents; that spoke of what the behavior of birds might mean, of what the color of the water said about the proximity of a river, words that were repeated for centuries, in harbors and on ships. They accompanied the fearful adventures of men who strayed ever further from their own coasts, sailing away into the black hole of the unknown, and returning—if they returned—with new maps of words, written up in the books of their memory. The estimated distance, the perilous gale, the position of the eternal stars, the comforting lee and the insatiable vortex; these verbal maps, passed on by word of mouth, were so vivid that nowadays sailors can still by them trace the wanderings of Odysseus.

The world had yet to be imprisoned in that spider's web of longitude and latitude, laced as it was with gossamer-thin, oh-so-straight lines, that stretched with geometric inevitability across the uncharted seas. Over there, where the coast was no longer visible, where the infinity of the sea reflected the infinity of the skies, that was where it was possible to fall off the world, an empty space where no one had yet ventured.

A few years ago I stood on the westernmost point of the island of Hierro, the most westerly of the Canary Islands, which was once at the very edge of the known world, until Columbus set sail into that infinity to search for Asia. In a decidedly theatrical gesture, the Spaniards have erected an enormous cross there and during my visit Nature added to the effect by painting a bloody sunset, complete with a raven on the right cross-beam. I could make out a tiny fishing boat in the distance and I remember feeling vaguely moved, perhaps on account of that tiny vessel in the vast emptiness, perhaps too because it was from those very islands that Columbus had set sail. The world then had only half a face.

A hundred years later, an anonymous artist and cartographer could render the world a face beneath a fool's cap, the face we still recognize. But for Columbus the other half of that face was still blank. Hierro, which would eventually come to lie directly on the perpendicular that could be dropped equidistant from the two bells of the fool's cap, then lay on the far left-hand side of his map. A quadrant, a ruler, and a pair of dividers were probably positioned next to it, the usual method of delimiting sea that had yet to be mapped, and which consequently on the portolan map of 1339 by Angelino Dulcert (Dolcino) of Mallorca is still portrayed as an empty expanse of brown parchment. Where the map stops, the loxodromic lines break off too. With the impassivity of pure science they appear to be straining to enter that mysterious region of folktale and legend.

There is a definite correlation between the emotion aroused by that physical point in space where I was standing, and the sight of this very early map, on which the world is barely recognizable. The northern countries appear to be clouded in a mist of conjecture, as if little progress had been made regarding these regions since the sketchy fragments of Strabo and Tacitus. Though it is possible to recognize the shape of the coasts of Italy and Spain, on my copy of the map you need a magnifying glass to decipher the names hemmed about those coasts in filigree writing. The Red Sea is red as blood, the Rhine flows westwards from Bohemia, a white elephant wanders near Nubia, and to see everything properly you have to keep turning the map around. The names are written upside down in relation to one another, as if the mapmaker was attempting, within that rectangle, to portray the roundness of the world. A Genoese map drawn 150 years later, with the Emperor of China upside down under the face of what could well be the North Wind, portrays the world as an ellipse full of mythical beasts, follies, sea monsters, monarchs, and enigmatic texts. At the same time, this quite unrecognizable depiction of the world is surrounded by an ocean, an ocean that by its supposed infinity afforded the possibility of sailing to Asia via the west. Forty years later Columbus was to do just that, encountering America along the way.

IN THE TALE by Borges we have met a map which is as huge as the country it portrays. But in the country where his story takes place, when they discover just how useless such a map is, they abandon it to "the rigors of Sun and Winter." In due course all that remains are "crumbling Fragments of Map inhabited by Beasts and Beggars." And yet, behind this superior form of lunacy lies a fundamental question: to what extent does a map of a specific region, or of the world, represent reality? In the case of those splendid old maps drawn up by the first great cartographers, we now know the sobering answer. In reality the continents had other shapes, the mythical creatures that rose up out of the sea or wandered the deserts did not exist, the world was a fairy tale, a fable, an inkling that grew more tangible, and therefore different, with each map.

Even so, it will never be possible entirely to dismiss misgivings about accuracy. A map of the Dutch East Indies hung on the wall at my old school. On it, the Dutch section of Borneo, now Kalimantan, was colored dark green, and I remember how, years later, when our plane was coming in to land above that extraordinarily green jungle, it felt as if that old school map was rushing toward me, getting larger by the minute, so that by the time we landed it literally corresponded to the world at my feet.

The map was correct in every way—after all, it was the twentieth century. Nothing had been left to chance or fantasy. But human beings will probably always hanker after the days when maps were paintings, with emperors, griffins, and unicorns, maps on which compass roses bloomed on seas sailed by no man, a time when every ship that put to sea returned with a different map to the one it had left port with. When, for a long while, the sheer scale of mystery dwarfed its resolution, and the world could still be decked out in a fool's cap.

2002

Nooteboom's Hotel 2

"NOOTEBOOM'S HOTEL 1" was written more than twenty years ago, and nothing has changed. I am still working on my hotel, that imaginary building that exists only inside my head, the hotel of the familiar and the far away, the city and the silence, of cold climes and warm. Nonexistent windows looking out onto paved-over squares and back gardens, parks and deserts. The beds float, the walls are made of the stuff that dreams are made of, the telephones communicate exclusively with one another, the rooms are made of air and I have written in each of them: books, letters, notes, stories, about the things, the places I saw. About towns and poems, books and exhibitions, traveling and photographs. I wrote about this traveling, which began almost fifty years ago and has always been about writing, reading, and especially *seeing*, in the essay, "The Eye of the Storm." And essentially I do not think that anything has changed. A nomadic life has, perhaps, taught me who I am and who I am not. This morning, in the first January month of a new century, I read a piece about a young Polish artist living in Amsterdam, who is working on a project she calls "Alienation," which entails her sleeping in a different hotel in this city each day for the coming sixty days, as an exercise in alienation, an *exercitatio spiritualis* that—who can say?—Ignatius Loyola might well have endorsed.

*   *   *

I AM NOT SURE I could put up with all the deliberation involved in such a project; I rather think I have been doing something similar all my life, but almost accidentally, simply by following my star. Nevertheless, it struck a chord with me, like an anonymous face in the crowd can strike a chord, a glance that catches your own and holds it, someone with whom you share something fundamental, without it ever being spelled out. Perhaps I should not assume the honorary title of nomad, after all I am no Tuareg, no medieval pilgrim making my way to Jerusalem or Santiago on foot, no Aboriginal trekking through the immeasurable void of the Australian outback, where I would perish of hunger and thirst in a very few days, because unlike them I cannot divine the miniscule, hidden signs of food and water. The poignancy that accompanies the sight of such people is difficult to put into words. The Spanish shepherd who makes use of still existent medieval paths to cover long distances with his flock during the transhumance, which takes place when the seasons change; the forlorn Aboriginal who, rejected by his tribe, alienated from his way of life, is washed up like driftwood on the fringes of the big city; the arrival of a desert caravan in northern Niger or Mali, after weeks of journeying; the expression in the eyes of an Italian friend when she arrived at the cathedral of Santiago de Compostela after walking for more than forty days. What they all have in common has to do with distance, and by this I do not just mean geographical distance, but the other sort as well, which has to do with remoteness and parting, detachment and estrangement. In Dutch, not only can one cover a distance, keep a distance, or create a distance, one can also distance *oneself*. Usually from a crowd, but sometimes also from certainty, safety, *stabilitas loci*.

This is often accompanied by confusion, anxiousness, and doubt. Even the experienced traveler can be afraid of sounds he does not recognize, just as he or she has to get used to the fact that every silence is different. Language that is not understood has a threatening or a seductive effect, inscrutable expressions can lead to misunderstandings that are unbridgeable, and all this is an integral part of the experience; indeed, one should not forget that every experience implies movement and repositioning.

This Polish woman aims to stay in sixty hotels in as many days: that will mean, as I know from experience, entering an unfamiliar space at least sixty times. People are good at hiding their emotions, from themselves too, but anyone who has ever studied how a cat checks out a space it has never seen before knows what is really going on. One way or another, that space has to be conquered. There are strategies and rituals for this, if only because the traveler, especially the lone traveler, knows, without really being aware of it, that in these alien surroundings he will surrender to that most unprotected human activity, sleep.

I can tell from my absurd collection of notepaper just how poetic those sleeping places were; Ang's Hotel in Brunei, Ti Eithne in Inishmore, Aggie Grey's Hotel on Samoa, Port Vila on Vanuatu, where I climbed up high to visit Robert Louis Stevenson's grave. Or the Dateline Hotel in Nuku'alofa on Tonga, the kingdom of islands in the Pacific, where the fictional time of our world divides into two, and the new millennium was proclaimed even though everywhere else the old one had not yet expired. All those names sing out from this yellowed writing paper, they record my bygone wanderings. Night has visited me in all those rooms, they have housed my dreams, both forgotten and remembered, and together with other obscure hotels in Burma, Niger, or Virginia, they now form part of that other, dreamed hotel, where it is hot and cold, where you may or may not be party to the appetites or miseries of your neighbor, but where, as now, the words always come to me that I take home on leaving.

In my novel *Rituals* I wrote: "It seemed that no one, not even the Pope, could wait for all those calloused years (etc.) to come to an end." Perhaps this was the reason why, when it finally drew near, I could not work myself up to feeling anything special. This did not really change until the final two weeks of that ruinous century—which had also been mine—when I met two men who had both in a sense kept themselves far removed from the hustle and bustle of the world, who had both lived, or were still living, in an elemental environment of stones and poverty, among people over whom the *Seinsvergessenheit* of the prophet from the Black Forest could have, as yet, no hold. How do you keep your distance from the world? In a Carthusian monastery, or among the anonymous millions of the city, there is no single recipe; the traveler too can build a wall around himself. But these two men, only one of whom I have actually met, had both chosen an island. The first one is Tim Robinson, who lived for a long time on Inishmore, the largest of the Aran Islands, just off the west coast of Ireland: a block of stone on which hardly anything grows, and upon which the ocean crashes with all the might it has been amassing since Newfoundland, so that it seems as though the end of the world is nigh. It is in another place that I have written about him, about *Stones of Aran*, the book he has written about the island. Two volumes, *Pilgrimage* and *Labyrinth*. One of Borges's stories tells of a king who wanted a map of his country drawn up. They set about the task, but not one of the maps was detailed enough for him, there were always places, roads, hills, streams that had been omitted, until eventually they ended up making a map that was as big as the country itself. Tim Robinson, a mathematician and painter, has done something similar with Inishmore. I know of no other book that professes to describe each yard of a particular area so breathtakingly: type of stone, plants, birds, legends, tradition, and, especially, names, which in this case means Gaelic names, a language which, upon this island, is itself apparently set in stone. I arrived during the last weeks of the last year, and it seemed as if I was driven there by the storm. The ferry between the mainland and Inishmore was sometimes practically at right angles to the inky-black sea, and each time the keel plunged downwards again, through the mist of spray and rain we would catch a glimpse of the vague contours of the island, rising and falling, shrouded, and I knew that each of the forms I saw there had a name that described and defined something. The previous evening, I had a long talk with the writer in a room, which itself appeared to be seaborne. Here was someone who had opted for a life that was the opposite of mine. He had remained in one place, a place of exceptional extremity, in a house where a sack weighted down with a stone served to keep the wind at bay; where there was no light except for a carbide lamp; on an island where, at that time, you could not buy bread, so you had to bake it yourself; where you were only accepted once you began to grow your own potatoes—on ground you had to create yourself, like some laborious deity, by placing layer upon layer of seaweed on the flat rocky ground, and sprinkling it with what little earth you had managed to scrape from the roots of hard, scrubby plants in the rock crevices.

How had he borne it, those twelve years?

By learning Gaelic, so that he could talk with the inhabitants, when they wanted to. And by keeping a diary, sometimes in ecstasy, sometimes in dreadful despair, the book from which his two volumes stem. And not forgetting Proust, the four thousand pages by that other hermit, who constructed *his* monastery in sophisticated, *fin-de-siècle* Paris. First in English, then in French, page for page, reading it aloud to his wife. And she? Studied Latin, read Virgil. And then Italian, Dante. The rewards and compensations of silence, a way of living, at one remove from the century, which had begun as a diversion. "But that diversion became my life." A tall, slim man, with something of the officer and the monk about him.

The other, much older, man resembled a monk too. I didn't see him in the flesh but on film, projected onto three screens simultaneously.

Zurich, a hotel whose rooms are named after writers. Which seemed to me very fitting for the last hotel of the century. I was given Canetti. His portrait had been painted above the bed, books by him lay about the room. He had not chosen me for company, but I was glad of his, and read what he wrote about the untimely death of his father, how inconsolable he was. I lost my father prematurely as well, during the war, and for a moment it was as if Canetti had written it for me, which of course he had: what is written is always for the one who reads it.

I had come to Zurich to view an exhibition about "The Oracle," but it was closed, which had definitely not been prophesied! Now I would have to see the century out sans maxims and omens. I walked through the snow to the Kunsthaus and entered a small cinema in which three screens were showing a triptych of three different films. "Three Windows." Another coast, another bare and barren landscape, more stones. An old man who resembles a Greek monk, another one. White hair. He feeds a cat, draws a circle, builds a wall of loose stones. He trudges endlessly along a stony track, into a visible eternity, it happens. A path like Petrarch's on Mount Ventoux, when he could not see the summit. On the other screens the sea, gray, everything gray, a misty film. I do not want to go in at first. I make out a few figures in the dimness, so decide to go and sit on the floor as well. There is a devotional atmosphere, which is not to my liking. Still too much restlessness—in me, that is. Not in the landscapes, nor in the man. The island is called Patmos; it is where John wrote the harsh, savage words of the Apocalypse. The man on the screens does not so much write, he draws. A circle. That irritates me. Then a few sentences, repeated over and over again, like a mantra. I ask myself why I find that circle so irritating. White paper, a felt pen, the simplest, most basic form, the old man's hand tracing that imperfect circle, as if he has thought of it for the first time. But when I begin to stand up I realize I want to stay sitting down. I don't know whether the others around me are experiencing the same thing, but everyone is keeping very still. The voice muses on, quiet but compelling, as if it is not meant for us. "Sounds come and go but the silence remains." Did I hear that then or only read it afterwards? "Silence, unbroken except for the odd sound, now and again. What is real is silence, dark silence. There's always something moving, a flash of light, a noise, but then it stops, and all that remains is dark silence. I wait in the darkness, in the rain, no sound besides the rain. Wait, not wait, do nothing, except wait. Do the shadows stir? Does the silence stir? No, they are not stirring, and neither am I. Are they waiting? I cannot tell . . ."

Later, when the spell has been broken, when I have learned that this man is Robert Lax, that he is eighty-five, that he used to belong to a traveling circus, and that the film has been made by two young Germans, I can still recall the feeling of stillness that gradually took possession of me. Harold Bloom once wrote that the Talmud warns that one should only read the Word when the light is such that the text reflects the shape of one's own face, *"Wenn das Licht so geneigt ist,"* it says in German, and this can be taken literally or figuratively. Recognition, and simultaneously irritation, on account of the reckless simplicity with which the circle was drawn, because that simplicity has to be earned, and because, during his long life, that old man in his meager room had presumably done just that, like the other man had used the years of his life to write the book which defined for ever the position of that life in relation to space and time. But what has actually happened here? For a moment, in a darkened auditorium in Zurich, I have recognized my own face in the script of a film, an unfinished, incomplete version of that unclouded old man's face on the screen before me.

In the eye of his storm it was infinitely more tranquil than it was in mine. I still had a long way to go. Once, possibly forty years ago, in a filthy, obscure hotel at the edge of the Sahara, near the border with Mauritania, I had been woken by the silence that man talked about. But it was not in fact the silence, it was fear, which had assumed the form of silence. I cannot describe it properly, because, like an animal, I had become that fear. I was not afraid of anything, because there was no room for anything. I remember the mud floor, something or other rustling, and how I went outside to the pitch-black heavens and the splendid immobility of all those stars. That night is written on my soul with a word I can no longer decipher. I subsequently chose the life which I now call my own, a way of life spent writing and recording in the apparent world, but how many words do you have to write in order to read just one?

1978

Publication Acknowledgments

"In the Eye of the Storm" was first published, with the title "In het oog van de storm," in *Nootebooms Hotel*, Uitgeverij Atlas, Amsterdam/Antwerpen, 2002.

"Forever Venice" was first published, with the title "Venetiaans Vignetten," in *Merian*, 5th May 1988 and as a New Year present in December 1998 by the Veen Uitgevers Groep.

"*Lady Wright* and Sir Jawara: a Boat Trip up the Gambia" was first published, with the title "*Lady Wright* and Sir Jawara en bootreis op de Gambia," in *Een avond in Isfahan. Reisverhalen*, Uitgeverij De Arbeiderspers, Amsterdam, 1978.

"Musings in Munich" was first published, with the title "Oeroude tijden," in *De wereld een reiziger*, Uitgeverij De Arbeiderspers, Amsterdam, 1978.

"The Stones of Aran" was first published, with the title "Araneilanden," in *Nootebooms Hotel*, Uitgeverij Atlas, Amsterdam/Antwerpen, 2002.

"Nooteboom's Hotel 1" was first published, with the title "Nootebooms Hotel 1," in *De wereld een reiziger*, Uitgeverij De Arbeiderspers, Amsterdam, 1978.

"At the Edge of the Sahara" was first published, with the title "Langs de Sahara," in *Bitter Bolivia/Maanland Mali*, De Bezige Bij, Amsterdam, 1971.

"That Earlier War: the Memorial in Canberra" was first published, with the title "In het huis van de vroegere oorlog," in *Vreemd water*, Uitgeverij De Arbeiderspers, Amsterdam, 1991.

"An Evening in Isfahan" was first published, with the title "Een avond in Isfahan," in *Een avond in Isfahan. Reisverhalen*, Uitgeverij De Arbeiderspers, Amsterdam, 1978.

"Upon Her Deads Bones They Built Mantua" was first published, with the title "Op haar dode gebeente bouwden zij Mantua," in *Waar je gevallen bent, blijf je*, Uitgeverij de Arbeiderspers, Amsterdam, 1983.

"Zurich" was first published, with the title "Zurich," in *Nootebooms Hotel*, Uitgeverij Atlas, Amsterdam/Antwerpen, 2002.

"Moonscape Mali" was first published, with the title "Maanland Mali," in *Bitter Bolivia/Maanland Mali*, De Bezige Bij, Amsterdam, 1971.

"When the World Wore a Fool's Cap" was first published, with the title "Toen de wereld nog een zotskap droeg," in *Nootebooms Hotel*, Uitgeverij Atlas, Amsterdam/Antwerpen 2002.

"Nootboom's Hotel 2" was first published, with the title "Nootebooms Hotel 2" in *De wereld een reiziger*, Uitgeverij De Arbeiderspers, Amsterdam, 1978.

The poem "The Gardener and Death" ("De tuinman en de dood") by P.N. van Eyck, translated by James Brockway, courtesy of the Foundation for the Production and Translation of Dutch Literature.